# THE CONSCIENTIOUS OBJECTOR

A Da Capo Press Reprint Series

# CIVIL LIBERTIES IN AMERICAN HISTORY

GENERAL EDITOR: LEONARD W. LEVY
*Brandeis University*

# THE CONSCIENTIOUS OBJECTOR

BY
WALTER GUEST KELLOGG

INTRODUCTION BY
NEWTON D. BAKER

DA CAPO PRESS • NEW YORK • 1970

A Da Capo Press Reprint Edition

This Da Capo Press edition of *The Conscientious
Objector* is an unabridged republication of the
first edition published in New York in 1919.

*Library of Congress Catalog Card Number 77-107412*

SBN 306-71893-6

Copyright, 1919, by Boni & Liveright, Inc.

Published by Da Capo Press
A Division of Plenum Publishing Corporation
227 West 17th Street, New York, N.Y. 10011
All Rights Reserved

Manufactured in the United States of America

# THE
# CONSCIENTIOUS
# OBJECTOR

BY
## WALTER GUEST KELLOGG
Major, Judge Advocate, U. S. A.
Chairman of the Board of Inquiry.

INTRODUCTION BY
## NEWTON D. BAKER
Secretary of War

# BONI AND LIVERIGHT
## NEW YORK                    1919

# PREFACE

Prior to my detail to the Board of Inquiry I had been reviewing, in the Office of the Judge Advocate General, the records of trial by court-martial of conscientious objectors. Although I had never set eyes on a conscientious objector, I firmly believed that they were, as a class, shirkers and cowards.

My first trip as a member of the Board upset most of my ideas regarding the objector. I began to see him in a new light. And an examination of over eight hundred objectors in twenty widely distributed military camps and posts has convinced me that they are, as a rule, sincere—cowards and shirkers, in the commonly accepted sense, they are not. Their sincerity, however, makes them no less a national problem.

What follows is an attempt to present the objector as he appears to a member of the Board. The opinions expressed are not to be taken as those of the Board or of my colleagues on the Board. It is a transcript of my personal impressions only, supplemented here and there by some of the literature of the subject.

One must see and talk with the objector in order to know him. The idealist who, without having visited a camp, writes so beautifully and sympathetically (not to say imaginatively) of him is hardly more to be trusted than is the bully who utterly condemns him without possessing himself, or appreciating in another, the conscience which so often informs and actuates his objections. The "C.O.", as the Army calls the objector, is not to be guessed at—one must know him to understand him.

Three things should be made plain. First, every class of objectors contains exceptions to my generalizations of that class. Every sect, as well, has its exceptions.

Second, I have endeavored to cover only those phases of the subject which came under my own observation. I have had nothing to do with the court-martialing of objectors; nothing to do with them after they had been tried by court-martial. As my duties and my experience with them began and ended with their examination, so begins and ends what I have written.

Third, I believe in freedom of thought and

expression of that thought. Peace is the desired thing and if it can be attained the sooner by a discussion of the ways and means of attaining it, all well and good. Talk, however, is one matter: action another. Many a man who wrote, argued and worked for peace was glad, when war came, to stop his talk and take up arms and fight for the peace which would not come otherwise. Of his type of citizenship no one can be but proud.

I am grateful to Majors Mark E. Guerin and Edgar Munson, of the Judge Advocate General's Department, for much criticism and suggestion.

W. G. K.

WASHINGTON, D. C.,
February 22, 1919.

# CONTENTS

x CONTENTS

# INTRODUCTION

The task of selecting an army of four million men, training it to the use of arms, equipping it and transporting half of it across the ocean to its field of battle, presented many difficult problems of organization. That these problems were solved in what must now seem a relatively short time is a credit to the genius of the American people for coöperation in the various fields of industry as well as an exhibition of the boundless resources of our country in manpower, material-power, and patriotic loyalty to the ideals upon which the Republic rests. The selection of such an army, in large part, by a non-volunteer process, presented another set of problems of quite a different kind, the solution of which appears only as negative results; but each of these problems was fraught with possibilities of consequences of a very affirmative character. In the long run we may say they were solved, because these problems affected the state of mind of the country, and as one looks back over the period of hostilities he finds the sentiment of the country sound and sure. That there was unanimity of judgment as to the correctness of all these solutions in the individual cases to which they were applied was quite too much to expect; but it may be said that throughout the whole period of the war the people of America accepted the sacrifices which the war entailed with rising spirit, that there was at no time any such disturbance of the public mind as suggested flagging adherence either to the cause of the country or to its vindication, whatever the cost.

When the obligation of military service was presented to millions of young men who were not permitted to elect whether they would serve or where they would serve in the Nation's cause, it was of course obvious that the call would be presented to men of every variety of religious belief and political opinion. The very freedoms guaranteed by our Constitution had engendered variety, while the population of America itself, differing from the populations of the countries of the old world, consisted of men of no one race with long and single traditions, but was a composite with men intermingled from all countries and with all periods of residence in and allegiance to America, from that of descendants of the early settlers to the recent attachments of the latest immigrants. The call to military service, therefore, was addressed to members of religious societies of ancient organization and settled creeds, to members of new religious groups formed to accent some particular phase of religious experience, and to men whose variance from accepted creeds was individual and personal; it was addressed to the learned and the illiterate; to the conservative, the liberal, the radical; to the native born, the foreign born; to those who had no conscious traditions except those of association with America, and to those whose roots ran back into the soil of the countries with which America was at war.

The men selected as a response to this call were to be welded into a homogeneous group; perhaps it is better to say they were to be called upon to subordinate the dominance of many philosophies and beliefs which would in times of peace seem most important and for which life-long sacrifices had been made, to the single principle of consecration to the death for the preservation of the one ideal of America and her institutions. For the most part, our young men were products of settled and usual communities, subjected to practically identical educational processes; all were of those years in which robust physical vitality is the normal characteristic, and as a consequence the new emotion, the chance to do something for one's country, easily called out an eager response.

Youth is the time of adventure; the opportunity to participate in an heroic undertaking, to measure strength with the best men in the world, to march under the banner of democracy and to die, if need be, for the right, quicken the pulse and strengthen the arm of the normal young American.

But this call also came to young men who had lived remote and apart from the stream of life, in small communities isolated from the rest of mankind by the observance of curious customs and devoting all their energy to the pursuit of certain ideals of religious or community organization which were held very sacred by the members of the community, but not understood, or at least not shared, by the rest of mankind. It came also to groups of men and to individuals whose political beliefs were idealistic and who, without definite religious basis, had on other grounds accepted non-resistance or some other principle as the corner-stone of a new civilization which to their heart's desire was to be free from ills which, in the old way, society had not yet overcome.

There were, therefore, human problems to be solved by those who organized this army. Every respect was to be shown constitutional guarantees; but something more than that was needed. The problem was to organize an army

and a country to fight a war, and the practical
answer to this question did not lie in formulæ
or phrases; the experience of history shows
that it did not lie in the passing of arbitrary
laws ruthlessly enforced, but rather, as the answer to every question in a democracy must lie,
in presentation to the people of the appeal of
duty and the recognition by the democracy of
the limitations which its own principles impose
upon arbitrary and passionate conduct.

The so-called "conscientious objector" is the
residuum left after this appeal is presented in
all of its forms and has had a chance to work
its effect. In every country in this war this
problem was presented. We do not yet know
all the answers that were attempted, but we do
know that in America out of many tens of thousands who claimed upon one ground or another
an irreconcilable objection to bearing arms or
serving in a military enterprise, there remained
at the end a very few hundred who persisted
and so found themselves in prison and protesting. To a very large number who presented
themselves in this attitude, mere contact with
their fellows was enough to enlarge their view
and bring them into harmony with the thought
of their generation. Other great numbers
found it impossible to bear arms, but not impossible to serve in non-military occupations

equally necessary and equally arduous. The little residue were of the most various types, and no one can have an intelligent opinion upon the problem presented by the "conscientious objector" who does not realize that some one person of his acquaintance can not be generalized so as to constitute the whole class included in the name. One's contempt for the slacker and the coward makes him naturally impatient of a man who refuses to take the risk of battle, and distrustful of excuses based upon conscience when one's own healthy conscience shows the path of duty to lie in the direction of self-sacrifice. But there is no sure way of being just in dealing with a problem of this kind except to take each "objector" as an individual, consider his antecedents, his opportunities, his limitations; and when these have all been weighed the judgment may be erroneous, but at least it has in it the ingredients of inquiry and patience which make it better than hasty assumptions.

Neither the Secretary of War nor the widespread officer group of a great army intent with every nerve upon training for the task of war could, in the nature of the case, give this patient, individual inquiry to these cases. It was clearly necessary to have specialists consider them, and with that end in view Major Richard

C. Stoddard, Dean Harlan F. Stone, and Judge
Julian W. Mack were made a Commission personally to examine into the questions presented
and the individuals affected. Major Stoddard
was later assigned to overseas duty, and Major
W. G. Kellogg assumed his place on the Commission. Major Kellogg's book is a detailed
account of the problem as he met it, and the
information which he sets forth will undoubtedly be valuable in helping us all to right think-
ing about conditions which affect our national
strength in times of stress. I have not had time
to attempt to weigh the opinions and conclusions
which Major Kellogg expresses, but I have a
strong belief that the Commission of which he
was a member enabled us with relative certainty to brush aside pretended scruples on the
one hand, and on the other to extend protection
to some defenseless and tragically burdened
people.

The up-shot of the whole inquiry, however, is
the emphasis which it gives to the task ahead
of us. The country was fortunate that the number of "conscientious objectors" was so small.
Our future strength depends upon our giving
such adequate opportunity for education, and
such demonstrations of the power and worth of
democracy as will preserve for us in the future
what was demonstrated in this war—a prac-

tically universal comprehension of the real meaning of our institutions and a national spirit which set even life itself below the preservation of liberty.

*Secretary of War*

# THE CONSCIENTIOUS OBJECTOR

## I

### THE OBJECTOR

No one of the collateral issues raised by the war has received greater attention than that presented by the conscientious objector. His virtues, as the virtues of one willing to undergo martyrdom rather than sacrifice an ethical principle, have been extolled by scores of writers who have represented him to the world as a man of education, ideals and almost prophetic vision. He has been eulogized by well-meaning persons, who understand neither the conscientious objector himself nor the national interest in a time of war, and he has, on the other hand, been roundly abused and reviled by a large part of our citizenry as a coward and a slacker. Apparently, there is no compromise ground: he is diabolically black to his critics while to his defenders his raiment is as the snows.

1

His friends early conceived it the duty of the Government first to care tenderly for the conscientious objector, and then, after this had been done, to wage, if possible, a successful war against Germany. His defamers were no less unreasonable in demanding that he and all others like him should be stood against a stone wall and shot. His protagonists invaded the magazines and clamored against the brutalities he had undergone; Vox Populi in the streets as loudly proclaimed that no treatment could possibly be too bad for him.

So much has been heard from him and of him since (and only since) the beginning of the war that the casual reader is apt to regard his problem as something distinctly novel. Indeed, the impression is current that the objector sprang into being with the Great War. He runs, however, far back into the history of the ages and his problem, so far from being a new one, has occupied the minds of many of the rulers of antiquity.

Mommsen, in his "Provinces of the Roman Empire", speaks of the Jews as having been exempted from war on account of their religious principles and the Jewish Encyclopedia tells us that "Marc Antony, at the request of Hyrcanus, exempted the Jews from service in the armies because they were not allowed to carry arms or to travel on the Sabbath. It was reserved for the Christian emperor Honorius to issue a decree—renewed by Theodosius, by Clotaire II and by the Byzantine emperors—forbidding Jews and Samaritans to enlist in the Roman army, probably in view of their Sabbath observances, as Dohm suggested.'' Sophocles created a noble type of objector in Antigone, who, refusing to follow the law of the State, illegally gave her brother burial and in so doing acted, as she said, in free obedience to ''the unwritten and unchanging laws of Heaven —laws that are not of to-day or yesterday but abide forever and of their creation knoweth no man.''

Gibbon, in the sixteenth chapter of ''The Decline and Fall of the Roman Empire,'' thus records the fate of two objectors in the third century: ''A sentence of death was executed upon Maximilianus, an African youth, who had been produced by his own father before the magistrate as a sufficient and legal recruit, but who obstinately persisted in declaring that his conscience would not permit him to embrace the profession of a soldier. It could scarcely be expected that any government should suffer the action of Marcellus the centurion to pass with impunity. On the day of a public festival, that officer threw away his belt, his arms and the ensigns of his office, and exclaimed with a loud voice that he would obey none but Jesus Christ the Eternal King, and that he renounced forever the use of carnal weapons and the service of an idolatrous master. The soldiers, as soon as they recovered from their astonishment, secured the person of Marcellus. He was examined in the city of Tingi  by the president of that part of Mauritania; and, as he was convicted by his own confession, he was condemned and beheaded for the crime of desertion.''

The Mennonites were exempted from military service in Holland in 1575; in Zeeland in 1577 and France, in 1793, accorded a similar exemption to the Mennonites of the Vosges, which exemption was confirmed by the great Napoleon, who employed them in hospital work on his campaigns. In the United States the members of certain religious denominations were exempted from general military service during the Civil War.

The history of the subject is important for present purposes only in so far as it shows that the problem persists and is recurrent. The question: What shall be done with the conscientious objector? has never yet received a satisfactory answer. Successive generations of men have been content, during each war, to temporize with the question, to devise some easily-workable scheme which half-solves, but does not solve. Some day, undoubtedly, a solution will be attained but that day will not come until the subject is given the thoughtful and sober consideration which it deserves. In the hurly-burly of war, expedients only can be devised and, amid all the busy concerns of peace, the problem of the objector will easily be forgotten only to present itself, in the event of a later war, as full of knots and perplexities as ever.

In Great Britain and in the United States the question was raised early in the war and received the serious, but necessarily hurried, consideration of the officials of each government. It is indisputable that in both countries some injustice has unwittingly been done: injustice alike to the objector who, in many instances, was unfairly treated and whose case was not infrequently misjudged, and injustice to the splendid soldiers of each country who, without any instinctive love of fighting in their breasts, were yet willing to enter the firing line, while these other men, no more God-fearing than they, were tamely suffered, because of their conscientious scruples, to engage in farming or in industrial work at home or, at the signing of the armistice, were being adequately maintained "over here" in comfortable camps by a paternalistic government. In so far as the war is over, the conscientious objector, as an administrative question, has disappeared.  The problem, however, has not been solved.  Now, if ever, there is time in which to consider it.

The number of men who present themselves as objectors is not, in comparison with the total draft, formidable.  Numerically, the problem indeed is of small importance; as a matter of principle it is of great importance.  The problem is to be fair to the minority without thereby being unfair to the majority.  A sovereign government must not oppress the honest objector nor, assuredly, should it grant him such special privileges that it thereby discriminates against its patriotic soldiery.

Great Britain and the United States have gone farthest in their efforts to do justice to the objector.  What treatment Germany and her allies have administered to the objectors is not known; it is said that they have been executed.  France has put some of them to death as "deserters;" France does not recognize objectors.  A responsible writer in one of the English magazines says:  "Great Britain exhibits a respect for individual conscience unknown to France, to Belgium and, I believe, to Italy and to most other continental countries."  The lot of the continental objector very probably has been not a happy one.

## II

GREAT BRITAIN, in her Military Service Act,
(5 & 6 Geo. Ch. 104-27 Jan. 1916), provides that
any man may apply for the issuance to him of
a certificate of exemption from the provisions
of the Act, "on the ground of a conscientious objection to the undertaking of combatant service." Such certificate may, in its terms, be absolute, conditional, or temporary, as seems best to
the authority who grants it, and may take the
form of an exemption from combatant service
only, or be conditional on the applicant's being
engaged "in some work which in the opinion of
the tribunal dealing with the case is of national
importance."

The Second Schedule to this Act established a
local tribunal for each local registration district,
which tribunal is to consist of from five to
twenty-five members. Any person aggrieved by
the decision of the local tribunal is entitled to
appeal to an "appeal tribunal," and a further
appeal is given, under certain conditions, from
the appeal tribunal to a central tribunal.

It has not yet been possible to obtain official figures as to the workings of this British system. Apparently, it has functioned with a fair measure of success, although it has been subjected to severe criticism. It is to be doubted if more substantial justice has been done in Great Britain than has been achieved in the United States under a less complicated system presently to be outlined.

Official data are lacking as to the number and disposition of men coming before the British tribunals. A writer in the "Manchester Guardian" (quoted in the "Literary Digest" of Aug. 31, 1918), states that 5,000 men refused to accept military service in England; 3,771 of these underwent one trial by court-martial, 623 were twice tried, 491 three times, 202 were tried four times, and 18 men were five times condemned to imprisonment at hard labor. These figures, it will be observed, are unofficial and, if correct, are correct only up to an unspecified time, presumably in 1918.

Among the better-known English objectors are Gilbert Cannan, the novelist; Francis Meynell, son of Alice Meynell; Stephen Hobhouse, whose father is the Right Hon. Henry Hobhouse and whose mother wrote the spirited appeal for the objector entitled "I Appeal Unto Cæsar"; and Clive Bell, the poet.

The British adopted a policy in their administration of military justice which has evoked widespread criticism. They have cumulated punishments for what, in all probability, is but one and the same offense. An objector A, who has received an exemption from combatant service, is, upon his induction into the army, ordered to dig a ditch. He considers this (wrongly, I believe) combatant service and refuses to obey. Tried by court-martial, he receives a sentence of imprisonment for, say, 112 days. He serves his sentence and, upon release, is returned to the army. Again the same or a like command is given, again he refuses, again he is tried and again he is sentenced, but this time to an imprisonment for perhaps two years. After he has served this second term, the process is repeated, but the third term may be for three years. If the war had continued, A's chances of ultimate liberty would have been increasingly small.

Great Britain, according to a writer in "The Survey", has not shot any of her objectors. "The death sentence has always been commuted into one of ten years penal servitude."

The English system of passing upon the sincerity of conscientious objectors differs from our own in that tribunals are constituted for every registration district, thus affording a readier hearing and a speedier disposition of the individual cases. Uniformity of policy or decision can hardly be attained by so many different local tribunals. The right of appeal given to the objector seems to assure to him a more thorough consideration of his contention; as a practical measure, however, the right of appeal makes the system of administration measurably more cumbersome and adds to the already tremendous burdens of the government. The various local tribunals doubtless have a personal familiarity with the different objectors coming before them and thus an extra-judicial knowledge of the facts in issue. In addition the procedure is more leisurely and, doubtless, in theory, at least, is more nearly adapted to secure substantial justice than the scheme used in the United States. In practice, it very probably has not achieved better results.

# III

## THE DOMINION OF CANADA

SECTION 11 of The Military Service Act of 1917 (7-8 George V) provides, among other things:

"(1) At any time before a date to be fixed in the proclamation * * * an application may be made, by or in respect of any man * * * called out by such proclamation, to a local tribunal established in the province in which any such man ordinarily resides, for a certificate of exemption on any of the following grounds:

\* \* \* \* \* \* \*

(f) That he conscientiously objects to the undertaking of combatant service and is prohibited from so doing by the tenets and articles of faith, in effect on the sixth day of July, 1917, of any organized religious denomination existing and well recognized in Canada at such date, and to which he in good faith belongs; and if any of the grounds of such application be established, a certificate of exemption shall be granted to such man.

(2) (a) A certificate may be conditional as to time or otherwise, and, if granted solely on conscientious grounds, shall state that such exemption is from combatant service only."

11

This, so far, is simple enough. To claim its benefits one must, first, himself conscientiously object to undertaking combatant service and, second, be prohibited from taking up combatant service by the tenets and articles of faith of some religious denomination as specified. "Conscientious scruples", as we know them, are not heeded—only "religious objections." The exemption is solely from combatant service.

In a Schedule appended to the Act are named several classes who, *as a matter of right,* are exempt from all service, whether combatant or non-combatant. Among these are: "7. Those persons exempted from Military Service by Order in Council of August 13th, 1873, and by Order in Council of December 6th, 1898." In these few words is the gist of much of Canada's troubles with the objector. The "persons" referred to are the "Western" Mennonites and the Doukhobors.

In 1872 certain Mennonites in Russia wished to settle in Canada. Canada, desirous that they should come, represented to them that they would be for all time absolutely free and exempt from military duties or service, either in time of peace or war. Canada offered them eight townships in Manitoba for their exclusive use and made most generous land grants and other provisions for them. In consideration of this "arrangement", as it is called, the Mennonites came to Canada and are now well distributed over the Northwest Provinces. There are about 45,000 in the Dominion.

After the passage of the Military Service Act, it was determined that Mennonites who had actually immigrated to Canada under the arrangement are entitled, wherever residing in Canada, to the benefits of the exemption, as, also, are their descendants, provided that they are bona fide members of the sect.

Many Canadian Mennonites had, prior to the war, made homes for themselves in the United States. After we entered the war, some of these Mennonites, fearful of being drafted into our own Army, returned to Canada for the purpose of availing themselves of the exemption contained in the Dominion Act. American Mennonites who had never set eyes on Canada now began to emigrate, in large numbers, to her western provinces. The Mennonites promptly became the bone of a national contention. To fix their status, an Order in Council was necessary, passed in October, 1918. This provided that only those Mennonites who had entered Canada under the arrangement, and their descendants who have *continuously* resided in Canada, are exempt. The Doukhobors gave rise to similar perplexities.

Canada thus exempts from (a) combatant service and (b), in stated cases, from both combatant and noncombatant service.* She has not recognized as an alternative "work of national importance", as has Great Britain, nor the farm or industrial furlough, as we have.

*Appendix IX.

# IV

IT will be well, in considering our own attempted solution of the problem, to hark back to the days of the Civil War, wherein the source of the law under which we have been proceeding is found in Section 17 of the Act of February 24, 1864 (13 Stat., 6, 9), which provided:

"Members of religious denominations, who shall by oath or affirmation declare that they are conscientiously opposed to the bearing of arms, and who are prohibited from doing so by the rules and articles of faith and practice of said religious denominations, shall, when drafted into the military service, be considered non-combatants, and shall be assigned by the Secretary of War to duty in the hospitals, or to the care of freedmen, or shall pay the sum of three hundred dollars to such person as the Secretary of War shall designate to receive it, to be applied to the benefit of the sick and wounded soldiers: *Provided,* That no person shall be entitled to the benefit of the provisions of this section unless his declaration of conscientious scruples against bearing arms shall be supported by satisfactory evidence that his deportment has been uniformly consistent with such declaration."

It is not easy to determine how well this statute worked out in practice. It is important to notice that its exemption is confined to "members of religious denominations" and "that satisfactory evidence" is required that their "deportment has been uniformly consistent with such declaration."

It could not have been difficult to decide as a matter of evidence whether a person was in fact a member of a specified religious denomination, which by the rules and articles of its faith was opposed to the bearing of arms, nor to ascertain whether or not his conduct had been uniformly consistent with the specific declaration which he had made. These matters are easily determinable as ordinary questions of fact and offer no such difficulties as are offered by the English and by our own statutes passed during the war. The Act is deficient, according to present day standards, in that it does not recognize the conscientious objector who does not happen to be a member of any certain religious denomination; i. e., the so-called "individual objector."

The first recognition of the conscientious objector by the United States since its declaration of war is contained in section 1644 of the Selective Service Law of May 18, 1917, which, after exempting certain public officials, ministers and students of religion, and persons in the military and naval services, provides:

"And nothing in this Act contained shall be construed to require or compel any person to serve in any of the forces herein provided for who is found to be a member of any well recognized religious sect or organization at present organized and existing and whose existing creed or principles forbid its members to participate in war in any form and whose religious convictions are against war or participation therein in accordance with the creed or principles of said religious organization; but no person so exempted shall be exempted from service in any capacity that the President shall declare to be noncombatant."

This law follows, in its wording and its obvious intent, the provisions of the law enacted during the Civil War. Had the law, as administered, remained in this form, it would have been comparatively easy to determine what classes of persons were entitled to its benefits.

It was, however, early recognized with the incoming of the drafts that the law as thus enacted was not sufficiently comprehensive. It made no provision for the large number of persons who, without claiming membership in any well-organized church, might be quite as conscientiously opposed to warfare as were any of the classes specifically mentioned therein. To remedy this defect, the President promulgated what is commonly known as "The Executive Order of March 20, 1918," in terms following:

GENERAL ORDERS, }   WAR DEPARTMENT,
No. 28.   } WASHINGTON, *March 23, 1918.*

The following Executive Order is published to the Army for the information and guidance of all concerned:

### EXECUTIVE ORDER.

1. By virtue of authority contained in section 4 of the act approved May 18, 1917, entitled "An act to authorize the President to increase temporarily the Military Establishment of the United States," whereby it is provided—

"And nothing in this act contained shall be construed to require or compel any person to serve in any of the forces herein provided for who is found to be a member of any well recognized religious sect or organization at present organized and existing and whose existing creed or principles forbid its members to participate in war in any form and whose religious convictions are against war or participation therein in accordance with the creed or principles of said religious organizations; but no person so exempted shall be exempted from service in any capacity that the President shall declare to be noncombatant."

I hereby declare that the following military service is noncombatant service:

(*a*) Service in the Medical Corps wherever performed. This includes service in the sanitary detachments attached to combatant units at the front; service in the divisional sanitary trains composed of ambulance companies and field hospital companies, on the line of communications, at the base in France, and with the troops and at hospitals in the United States; also the service of supply and repair in the Medical Department.

(*b*) Any service in the Quartermaster Corps, in the United States may be treated as noncombatant. Also, in rear of zone of operations, service in the following: Stevedore companies, labor companies, remount depots, veterinary hospitals, supply depots, bakery companies, the subsistence service, the bathing service, the laundry service, the salvage service, the clothing renovation service, the shoe repair service, the transportation repair service, and motor-truck companies.

(c) Any engineer service in the United States may be treated as noncombatant service. Also, in rear of zone of operations, service as follows: Railroad building, operation and repair; road building and repair; construction of rear line fortifications, auxiliary defenses, etc.; construction of docks, wharves, storehouses and of such cantonments as may be built by the Corps of Engineers; topographical work; camouflage; map reproduction; supply depot service; repair service; hydraulic service; and forestry service.

2. Persons ordered to report for military service under the above act who have (a) been certified by their Local Boards to be members of a religious sect or organization as defined in section 4 of said act; or (b) who object to participating in war because of conscientious scruples but have failed to receive certificates as members of a religious sect or organization from their Local Board, will be assigned to noncombatant military service as defined in paragraph 1 to the extent that such persons are able to accept service as aforesaid without violation of the religious or other conscientious scruples by them in good faith entertained. Upon the promulgation of this order it shall be the duty of each Division, Camp, or Post Commander, through a tactful and considerate officer, to present to all such persons the provisions hereof with adequate explanation of the character of noncombatant service herein defined, and upon such explanations to secure acceptances of assignment to the several kinds of noncombatant service above enumer-

ated; and whenever any person is assigned to noncombatant service by reason of his religious or other conscientious scruples, he shall be given a certificate stating the assignment and reason therefor, and such certificate shall thereafter be respected as preventing the transfer of such persons from such noncombatant to combatant service by any Division, Camp, Post, or other Commander under whom said person may thereafter be called to serve, but such certificate shall not prevent the assignment of such person to some other form of noncombatant service with his own consent. So far as may be found feasible by each Division, Camp, or Post Commander, future assignments of such persons to noncombatant military service will be restricted to the several detachments and units of the Medical Department in the absence of a request for assignment to some other branch of noncombatant service as defined in paragraph 1 hereof.

3. On the first day of April, and thereafter monthly, each Division, Camp, or Post Commander shall report to the Adjutant General of the Army, for the information of the Chief of Staff and the Secretary of War, the names of all persons under their respective commands who profess religious or other conscientious scruples as above described and who have been unwilling to accept, by reason of such scruples, assignment to noncombatant military service as above defined, and as to each such person so reported a brief, comprehensive statement as to the nature of the objection to the acceptance of such noncombatant military service entertained. The Secretary of War will from time to time classify the persons so reported and give further directions as to the disposition of them. Pending such directions from the Secretary of War, all such persons not accepting assignment to noncombatant service shall be segregated as far as practicable and placed under the command of a specially qualified officer of tact and judgment, who will

be instructed to impose no punitive hardship of any kind upon them, but not to allow their objections to be made the basis of any favor or consideration beyond exemption from actual military service which is not extended to any other soldier in the service of the United States.

4. With a view to maintaining discipline, it is pointed out that the discretion of courts-martial, so far as any shall be ordered to deal with the cases of persons who fail or refuse to comply with lawful orders by reason of alleged religious or other conscientious scruples, should be exercised, if feasible, so as to secure uniformity of penalties in the imposition of sentences under Articles of War 64 and 65, for the wilful disobedience of a lawful order or command. It will be recognized that sentences imposed by such courts-martial, when not otherwise described by law, shall prescribe confinement in the United States Disciplinary Barracks or elsewhere as the Secretary of War or the reviewing authority may direct, but not in a penitentiary; but this shall not apply to the cases of men who desert either before reporting for duty to the military authorities or subsequently thereto.

5. The Secretary of War will review the sentences and findings of courts-martial heretofore held of persons who come within any of the classes herein described, and bring to the attention of the President for remedy, if any be needed, sentences and judgments found at variance with the provisions hereof.

WOODROW WILSON.

THE WHITE HOUSE,
        *20 March, 1918.*
    [383.2, A. G. O.]
BY ORDER OF THE SECRETARY OF WAR:
                    PEYTON C. MARCH,
            *Major General, Acting Chief of Staff.*

OFFICIAL:
> H. P. McCAIN,
> *The Adjutant General.*

Section 3 of this order, in using the words "religious *or other conscientious scruples*" recognized equally the objector who belonged to a religious sect or organization opposed to war and the objector who did not belong. From then on, the two classes were accorded like treatment: the "religious objector" and the "individual objector."

The order, despite certain obscurities, was obviously meant to secure to every objector fair and considerate treatment. Conceived in a broad and liberal spirit of toleration, it is in line with, but more progressive than, the policy adopted during the Civil War. In its recognition of the "individual objector" and in its general intent, it is similar to the British Act.

A series of instructions issued by the Secretary of War further regulated the treatment to be accorded to objectors.* It was early ruled that men accepting service in noncombatant branches would not have to bear sidearms; that Mennonites should not be required to wear the uniform, "as question of raiment is one of the tenets of their faith." The instructions from time to time were changed and amplified as cir-

* Appendix VII.

cumstances demanded. On June 1, 1918, the Secretary appointed a Board of Inquiry, whose duty it was to examine into the sincerity of the conscientious objectors brought before it.

The Secretary also issued, "as authoritative interpretations of paragraph three, General Orders No. 28, War Department, 1918" (i. e., of paragraph three of the Executive Order quoted), the following summary:

(a) As a matter of public health every man in camp, entirely apart from his military status, shall be expected to keep himself and his belongings and surroundings clean, and his body in good condition through appropriate exercise. Men declining to perform military duties shall be expected to prepare their own food.

(b) If, however, any drafted man, upon his arrival at camp either through the presentation of a certificate from his local board, or by written statement addressed by himself to the commanding officer, shall record himself as a conscientious objector, he shall not, against his will, be required to wear a uniform or to bear arms; nor, if, pending the final decision as to his status, he shall decline to perform, under military direction, duties which he states to be contrary to the dictates of his conscience, shall he receive punitive treatment for such conduct. He shall be required to furnish such information and to render such assistance as may be necessary to complete the original entries on all records relating to his induction into the service; but will be informed that such action on his part will not, in any way, prejudice his status as a conscientious objector.

(c) No man who fails to report at camp, in accordance with the instructions of his local board, or who, having reported, fails to make clear upon his arrival his decision to be regarded as a conscientious objector, is entitled to the treatment outlined above.

(d) In the assignment of any soldier to duty, combatant or noncombatant, the War Department recognizes no distinction between service in the United States and service abroad.

Three or four of the many instructions were issued to the service as "confidential." * Had they been made public they might have been the means of creating even more objectors.

* Appendix VII.

# V

THE Board of Inquiry, constituted by the Secretary of War on June 1, 1918, was composed of a representative of the Judge Advocate General's Department (Major Richard C. Stoddard) as chairman, Julian W. Mack, Judge of the United States Circuit Court of Appeals, and Harlan F. Stone, Dean of the Columbia University Law School. The Board immediately began the examination of the objectors in the different Army camps in this country. Major Stoddard continued as chairman until about the middle of August, 1918, when he was detailed for duty overseas. He was succeeded by the present writer; the civilian members have remained.

The Board was appointed solely to inquire into and to determine the sincerity of conscientious objectors. Its function primarily was to examine all objectors, not under charges, who had declined to accept noncombatant service, or who had not been assigned to noncombatant service by their camp commander, because, in the judgment of the camp commander, they were insincere.

Although this was the original purpose of the Board, it later, with the consent of the camp commander, examined such men as were under charges and had not been brought to trial. Its findings were merely advisory to the Secretary. The Board not infrequently, on its own motion or on the motion of the objector, granted a rehearing in doubtful cases.

The work of the Board was essentially migratory in character. At various times the War Department has had under consideration the concentration of the objectors at one or two army posts, and, had this been done, the duties of the Board would have been performed with far more despatch and its resulting labors would have been greatly reduced, but so many more important duties required the attention of the Department that this plan of concentration was never adopted. It therefore remained the duty of this Board, composed of three members, to journey from one end of the country to the other—from Camp Devens in Massachusetts, for example, to Camp Kearney in California, from Camp Lewis in the state of Washington to Camp Gordon in Georgia—to all camps, north, east, south and west, in which objectors were quartered. The travel thus imposed upon the

Board consumed a vast amount of time and added considerably to the work involved.

The difficulty of determining the sincerity with which a conviction is held must be apparent to all. It is to plumb the depths of a man's mind with the purpose of finding if truth is at the bottom. Had the task been entrusted to a similar board of three men who were to function within a registration district, for instance, its method of work might have been different, and the results achieved more satisfying. If more evidence could have been taken, if the issues had been capable of documentary proof or proof by additional witnesses, one would feel that its decisions had been more often right. The Board, however, had difficulties of time and of space to contend with; it examined a large number of men with expedition and its work was probably as well done as the work of any small board covering so broad a territory.

The Board was consistent in its methods and its decisions. All objectors came before one and the same Board. Had there been a dozen boards, widely different results might have been reached in very similar cases, as witness the divergent sentences imposed by locally constituted courts, both civil and military.

The work was done as convenience demanded; with the entire Board sitting in a case, or, with two members, or even, as often happened, with one member, sitting as the Board. The extent of the examination varied with the facts presented. If the objector belonged to a well-recognized religious sect, such as the Mennonites or the Quakers, it was necessary to ascertain when he became a member of that church, and to find if he had a certificate from his Local Board.* The production of such a certificate was evidence that his Local Board believed him to be a bona fide religious objector. If he had joined before April 6, 1917, the date of our entrance into the war, if it was apparent that he had been a consistent member of the church, regular in attendance and adhering to its doctrines, only a few collateral questions were asked, such for example as concerned his business, his family connections, his habits, his conduct since entering camp, his attitude toward the use of force, his feelings about Germany and our participation in the war. If his answers were satisfactory and if he was in appearance and bearing an honest man, the Board was likely to find him sincere in his objections and to recommend him for the prescribed exemptions. Oftentimes something would develop in his testimony which would create suspicion; in such

* Appendix VIII.

cases, the examination would be greatly prolonged.

The individual objector, who based his convictions upon the Bible and yet belonged to no
church, presented a more troublesome problem.
Such a man was examined at length with the
purpose of finding out, if possible, how intimate
his acquaintance with the Bible was and for how
long such intimacy had been maintained; the
specific passages therein which had influenced
him, and his understanding and interpretation
of those passages. Some men were found who
had been members originally of such churches
as the Methodist, the Catholic, or the Baptist,
but, having abandoned their church, had become
non-sectarians. These men based their present
objections to warfare upon the Bible as a
whole or upon certain verses or chapters in the
Bible.

The political objector, such as the Socialist,
gave the greatest difficulty. The objector who
happened to disagree with the Congress or with
the President regarding our entrance into
this particular war clearly did not come within
the Congressional enactment requiring that the
objection be "against *warfare in any form.*"
The number of these men encountered was in-
considerable, and yet one recalls several who
testified that they would have fought in the Civil

War, who acknowledged that they would have participated in the Russian Revolution, but who, for some reason or other, said they could not conscientiously take any part in this war. In these cases it was held that such a person was not a conscientious objector within the terms of the law and the various orders. On the other hand, Socialists were encountered whose teachings, although basically economic, had yet become so ingrained within them as to be a matter of conscience that warfare in any form was absolutely wrong. The examination of such a man was protracted and covered, as far as possible, the attitude of the objector to every conceivable subject bearing upon the war and his relation to it.

An order issued March 6, 1918, directed that a psychological examination should be made of all conscientious objectors. This examination, as usually conducted, covered a wide range, and was intended to reach into the utmost recesses of the objector's mind. The objector was given a rating psychologically, and any inconsistencies in his testimony were noted, and submitted to the Board upon its visitation. The officers in command of the objectors, who had had them under close observation for months, were often helpful to the Board by reports, which they submitted in writing or gave orally, regarding the history of the men about to be examined.

The Board classified objectors as follows:

1-A. Those found to be sincere religious objectors, and recommended for farm or industrial furlough.

1-B. Those found to be sincere non-religious objectors, and recommended for farm or industrial furlough.

1-C. Those found to be sincere conscientious objectors, who are recommended for the Friends' Reconstruction Unit.

2-A. Those found to be sincere conscientious objectors as to combatant, but not sincere as to noncombatant service, and who are therefore recommended to be assigned to noncombatant service.

2-B. Those found to be sincere conscientious objectors who are willing to accept, and who are therefore recommended for, noncombatant service.

2-C. Those found to be sincere conscientious objectors, who are willing to accept service in and who are assigned to, reconstruction hospitals.

3. Those found to be insincere and assignable to any military duty.

4. Those objectors who are recommended to be sent to Fort Leavenworth, Kansas, for further examination.

5. Those objectors who, upon examination, withdraw their objections.

6. Those found to be sick or unfit for examination, and recommended to be sent to a hospital for treatment.

7. Alien enemies or neutrals.

8. Those objectors who are recommended for mental examination and discharge, if not found competent.

9. Not in camp—not seen by the Board.

10. Under criminal charges—the Board expresses no opinion until the decision of the court.

11. Tried by court-martial, therefore no opinion is now expressed.

The Friends' Reconstruction Unit was organized by the Friends or Quakers for reconstruction work in France. Its purpose is to rebuild the devastated villages, to provide and care for their women and children, and, generally, to upbuild France and its civil morale. It is in no way connected with the military establishment, and the objector, if deemed worthy of such service, understood that he was not to be under military control, except in so far as it was necessary that the Government should grant him a furlough or leave of absence, which the Government at any time could terminate for cause.

The reconstruction hospitals appealed to many who were unwilling to accept the usual noncombatant services. These hospitals were designed, not to refit men for purposes of combat, but only to reconstruct or rehabilitate soldiers so badly maimed or wounded that they would never be able to return to the firing line. Such hospitals were to refit men for civil life.

# VI

THE objectors examined by the Board professed membership in an astonishing number of different sects and denominations, the names of most of which are unfamiliar to the average layman. The different denominations include: Mennonites, The Society of Friends or Quakers, Plymouth Brethren, The International Bible Students Association or Russellites, Dunkards or German Baptist Brethren, Seventh Day Adventists, Church of God and Saints of Christ, Disciples of Christ, Church of Christ, Church of Daniel's Band, Church of the Living God, Pentecostal Church of the Nazarene, True Light, Metropolitan, Molokans, Christians, Brethren in Christ, Christadelphians, Church of the First Born, Israelites of the House of David, Church of the Holiness, Koreshan Unity, Zionists and a score of others.

It will perhaps be well to consider briefly some of the outstanding types of certain of these sects. The Mennonites, the Quakers, and the Molokans present the most interesting features.

The Mennonites comprise the largest class of conscientious objectors; the Quakers, perhaps the most admirable. The Molokans undoubtedly, not because of their number, but because of their novelty, have been among the most perplexing cases with which the War Department has had to deal.

### THE MENNONITES

Prior to my detail to the Board of Inquiry I had never seen a Mennonite and I had heard of them only casually. It is, therefore, to be assumed that I speak of them with no prejudices, except, possibly, with the prejudices that I have derived from the examination of large numbers of them. I understand that the Mennonites maintain several colleges; that many of their members are good citizens and entitled to all respect as such, and I have glanced through various histories of the Mennonite Church, written by Mennonites, from which I can believe that the church has very many traditions of which it may well be proud. I have not met any Mennonites except those who have come before the Board of Inquiry as conscientious objectors, and it should be understood that, in speaking of the sect, I am speaking only of the comparatively few of them who have been examined by the Board.

The Mennonites take their name from one Menno Simons, who was born in Friesland in the year that Columbus discovered America. One Abbe Philipsz is regarded as the actual founder of the church, which had its origin in Zurich about the year 1523. The Mennonites, according to the Encyclopedia Britannica, discard the sacerdotal idea and acknowledge no authority outside the Bible and the enlightening conscience. They limit baptism to believers and lay stress on those precepts which vindicate the sanctity of human life and a man's word.

Non-resistance has long been one of the foundation stones of their faith. At a general conference of the Mennonites held at Dort, Holland, in 1632, a compilation was made of their previous confessions of faith and called "A Declaration of the Chief Articles of our Common Christian Faith." The Declaration contains this, in substance: "Christ has forbidden His followers the use of carnal force in resisting evil and the seeking of revenge for evil treatment. Love for enemies cannot be shown by acts of hatred and revenge but by deeds of love and good will." This doctrine is accepted today by the majority of Mennonites.

The Mennonites, as hitherto noted, were exempted from military service by the great Napoleon and others, and certain classes have, as a body, received exemption from the Canadian Government.

A psychologist, who obtained statistics on 1060 cases taken from twelve Army camps, informs me that 554 of those cases were Mennonites. My own observation would lead me to believe that even a larger percentage of the objectors examined by the Board of Inquiry were Mennonites.

Germany, in the eighteenth century, forbade the Mennonites to hold land, because of their opposition to military service. Catherine II of Russia, in order to induce them to immigrate, promised the Mennonites huge territories in her empire where they would be permitted to live according to their own religion and customs. In acceptance of her offer, thousands of them left Prussia in 1788 and established colonies in southern Russia.

In 1870 the Imperial Russian Government imposed a ten-year limit to their exemption from service, but provided that any of them were free to leave Russia, if they desired, within the ten years. Between 1874 and 1880 more than 15,000 migrated from Russia to America. This wholesale going alarmed the Imperial Government, negotiations with the Mennonites were begun and a decision was reached that thereafter they could perform their military duties ''in the forestry of the State"—work very probably similar to that done by our Engineer Corps.

The faith first settled in the United States in 1683, the members having been brought here by William Penn's offer of religious liberty. In 1916 the church had 79,363 members here, with 1398 ministers and 838 organizations. They are divided into sixteen bodies or orders of which the most prominent are: The Mennonites, Amish Mennonites, General Conference Mennonites, Reformed Mennonites, Defenseless Mennonites, and Old Order of Amish Mennonites. Their members come largely from Pennsylvania, Ohio, Indiana, South Dakota, Illinois and Iowa, but some are doubtless to be found in almost every state of the Union. There are more Mennonites in this country than in any other country in the world.

They are distinctly an agricultural people and live, for the most part, in isolated farming communities. The majority of them joined the church in early manhood, and testify that they have attended church since childhood with their mothers and fathers, sisters and brothers. The objector's father and mother, his grandfather and grandmother, and his even more remote ancestors, have commonly been devout Mennonites. They marry among themselves and have unusually large families. Their ancestry is very often German. They are a thrifty, hard-working, prosperous people.

The Mennonite is possessed of singular characteristics. His hair and beard are unkempt—if he is an Old Amish Mennonite he explains that it is against his religious principles to cut his hair or to trim his beard. Leviticus 19.27 he takes with absolute literalness: "Ye shall not round the corners of your heads, neither shalt thou mar the corners of thy beard." He is, of course, not in uniform. His trousers open only at the side and do not button, but hook together. He wears no jewelry of any kind. He shuffles awkwardly into the room—he seems only half awake. His features are heavy, dull and almost bovine.

He very probably does not speak English with any degree of even colloquial fluency—he is almost certain to speak German, and German, or Pennsylvania Dutch, is the language of his family circle and of his church. He rarely has received any education beyond the fourth or fifth grade. He has never held public office of any kind, and takes no interest in the social life of his community. He cares nothing about good roads or any form of social uplift, and, in most cases, he has never voted. He is not interested in voting. He will perhaps, tell you that he has "led a sinful life", and when you inquire into the particular variety of vice that he has practiced, you find that on one or two occasions he has attended moving pictures, which he seems to think are very wrong indeed. You can not get him to say whether in his opinion the United States should triumph over Germany or Germany over the United States—he will tell you, "It is not for me to judge." He will, in all likelihood, testify that if some brute were to break into his mother's or sister's room and attempt to rape her, he would allow his mother or sister to be raped before he would shoot or otherwise injure her assailant. He will not admit having been in any fight or having ever used force against a human being since joining the church.

He professes to be a great reader of the Bible and is capable of disclosing a surprising knowledge of its contents. He takes "Thou shalt not kill" and similar passages with absolute literalness, and any verse which seems to favor warfare he will explain as possessing a figurative intention. His Bible, well thumbed, is surely somewhere in his deep pockets, and he can turn readily to almost any chapter that may be in question.

I had spent some time in examining Mennonites concerning the sinking of the *Lusitania,* but nothing significant developed from my questioning: many of them were equally unsatisfying when asked regarding General Foch and Edith Cavell. It occurred to me one day to ask a Mennonite what the *Lusitania* was. He did not know! He had, he told me, never heard of Edith Cavell, nor of General Foch, nor, strange to say, of General Pershing. Nor, I later ascertained, was his case an exception. I have examined at least fifty Mennonites at random in widely separated camps who did not know what the *Lusitania* was, who Edith Cavell was, nor who General Foch or who General Pershing is. Others had heard of the *Lusitania*—that she was a boat which they *thought* had been sunk by the Germans, but they knew nothing about the surrounding facts. Several thought her an American ship; one said "she had got into a glazier (sic) of ice." Two or three had an idea that "Edith Cavell was some nurse who was shot." About half of them had heard of General Foch; one said he was "the manager of the French army." Pershing was more familiar; he was "the American general" or, as several of them put it, "one of the big men in the American army."

Such ignorance, to one who has seen many of them, is hardly surprising. They are an isolated people; they do not mix freely with others. They remain now as their forefathers were three centuries ago. They are concerned little with what the world thinks and does; they read no newspapers other than their village weekly, which is not unlikely to be printed in German. Civilization, apparently, has passed them by; the twentieth century has hopelessly outdistanced them. They remain a curious and an alien survival of an old-world people, an anachronism amid the life of to-day.

The Mennonite faith may derive much from the inheritance of the ages, but a considerable body of the Mennonites surely need serious consideration, both by their church authorities and by the Government. It is difficult to realize that we have among our citizenry a class of men who are so intellectually inferior and so unworthy to assume its burdens and its responsibilities. I doubt extremely if fifty per cent of the Mennonites examined, because of their ignorance and stupidity, ever should have been admitted into the Army at all; I am certain that ninety per cent of them need a far better preparation for citizenship than they have ever received. They are good tillers of the soil; they are, doubtless, according to their lights, good Christians, but they are essentially a type of Americans of which America cannot be proud.

The problem of the conscientious objector, as applied to the Mennonites, is particularly and

forcefully one of education, not more in the
rudiments of schooling than in the inculcating
of the social and national spirit.

### THE FRIENDS, OR QUAKERS

It is pleasant now to turn to The Society of
Friends.  My previous acquaintance with the
Quakers was almost as meager as my acquaintance with the Mennonites.  However much it
may be regretted that so intelligent and so,
at bottom, patriotic a class of citizens should
differ so radically from most of us as regards
duty in a time of war, the Quaker, taken by and
large, is fundamentally sincere.

I think of the majority of the Quakers that I
have seen as pleasant-appearing, clean-limbed
young men.  They knew and understood the
causes of the war, they were well versed in current events, and they balked only at actual fighting.  A large part of them desired noncombatant
service.  Many had some months before put in
an application for service in the Friends' Reconstruction Unit, the acceptance of which was
subject to the finding of the Board of Inquiry.

They understood the dangers and were willing and anxious to risk all of them.  A Quaker
told me that an aerial bomb had been dropped
upon one of the Units in France and had killed
or severely wounded twenty-two of its members,

and yet it in nowise dampened his ardor to serve.

The spirit of the Friends, though we may attribute it to an inherent narrowness, is yet a brave spirit, prompted by a genuine intelligence and backed by a fine sincerity. And what has been said holds true of at least a very large majority of the Quakers I have examined—I cannot now recall an exception.

### THE MOLOKANS

Six objectors styling themselves "Molokans", or "Holy Jumpers" were quartered in one of the middle-western camps. I was told that they were on a so-called "hunger strike," absolutely refusing to take food or drink, and that this hunger strike was intended by them solely to embarrass the camp authorities. The officer in charge had ordered that they be taken to the base hospital to be forcibly fed. The officer asked what I thought of this course. I answered that it seemed to me that to send these men to a base hospital was merely to notify them that the camp was afraid of them and their strike, and that I, in his place, would return them to quarters and pay no attention to their hunger strike beyond putting food and water within their easy reach. If they did not, within a reasonable time, use this food and water, and if their physical condition became debilitated so that other measures were necessary to save their lives, it would then be advisable to send them to a base hospital and there to consider what should be done.

Upon examining them, the nature of their hunger strike became evident. Only one of them spoke English, and he testified that they all, at different times, had come to this country from Russia, had settled first in California and then had migrated to Arizona. All were married and had large families, and each was working a farm which he had bought on contract. He said further that they were all Molokans, and that their parents before them had been Molokans. They did not believe in fighting or taking part in warfare in any form. Their church had always taught non-participation in war.

The Holy Spirit, he said, at intervals visited them and gave them spiritual guidance. When the Holy Spirit was upon them, they involuntarily jumped about and from this they had derived the name of "Holy Jumpers." He said that two years before the Selective Service Law was enacted, the Holy Spirit came to them and informed them that two years later the United States would pass a draft act for the purpose of waging a war; that the Holy Spirit told them that they must not register under the draft and must have nothing to do with the war in prospect, as war of any kind was wrong. About two years later, exactly as the Holy Spirit had foretold, the draft law was passed. The six Molokans then went before their Local Boards, told the Boards that the Holy Spirit had forbidden them to register, and each left with his Local Board his name and address. They later were inducted into the service as draft evaders and spent about a year in confinement. Upon their release they were brought to camp and, in course of time, appeared before the Board of Inquiry.

The English-speaking Molokan informed the Board that they did not wish to embarrass the Government in any way, but that they could not take any part in the war and could not accept even noncombatant service. They were unwilling to take even a farm furlough because that, too, was under military control. When informed that such a refusal would undoubtedly subject them to charges and to further imprisonment, they said it did not matter—that they would willingly be shot to death before they could do anything under the Government for the prosecution of the war. He asserted that his father had seen some of his ancestors shot down in Russia for refusing to be conscripted and that they themselves would much rather suffer imprisonment or death than violate their religious convictions.

Their religion compelled them to be vegetarians. They said they had never eaten any flesh food and that they always prepared their own food so that they could make sure that their vegetables had not been cooked in a vessel which had contained animal fats. They protested that they had started no hunger strike with the idea of embarrassing the Government, but only desired that they be allowed to cook their own kind of food in the way prescribed by their church.

They were given a prolonged examination and, so far as I could determine, were absolutely sincere in their convictions. All that the Board could do for them was to recommend that they be granted a farm or industrial furlough and this they refused to accept. It was suggested that more vegetables should be given them and that they should be allowed to do their own cooking.

In this country, little seems to be known of the Molokans. From the testimony adduced, it would appear that there is quite a colony of them in southern California and in Arizona; their spokesman claimed there were 20,000 or more Molokans in the United States.

The proper name of these people seems to be *Molokane* and they are so called because they drink milk (*moloko*) during their fasts. In Stepniak's "The Russian Peasantry", it is said that the Molokans are strict Christians of the Protestant type, who seceded from the Dukhoborzy during the last quarter of the eighteenth century and that they strictly object on religious grounds to the profession of arms. In 1826 Nicholas I of Russia issued a ukase that all able-bodied Dukhoborzy and Molokane should be enrolled in the Army and that those unqualified for military service should be exiled to Siberia. It was found that the able-bodied Molokane did not object to the peaceful every-day duties of service, but "when brought face to face with the enemy, threw their arms to the ground and refused to march or to fire. The most awful corporal punishment could not make them obedient, so that after a time the Commander of the Caucasian army was compelled to pray the emperor not to send him any Dukhoborzy or Molokane." It should be remembered in reading this that it is a Russian who uses the phrase: "the most awful corporal punishment."

Stepniak calls the Molokane "the most intellectually developed body among the whole of our rural population." The Molokans seem to have been a thorn in the flesh of the Russian government, and the few who announced themselves here as objectors have been most perplexing.

Whether the six Molokans truthfully represented their religion is not known, but, during the
time that the Board had them under observation, they appeared to be absolutely sincere, and
of more than average intelligence. They very
probably were good fathers and model husbands
whose good citizenship could hardly be questioned until they and their exotic religion were
brought plump against the grim realities of
war.

### THE COLORED OBJECTOR

The colored objectors have not been numer-
ous; it is doubted if more than fifteen or twenty
have been before the Board for examination.
Taken as a whole, they more nearly approach
the fanatical type than any others examined.
They were by no means unintelligent, and a
glibness of speech was the distinguishing fea-
ture of their testimony. Only an exceptionally
able stenographer could "take" the majority of
them and it is safe to say that six court stenog-
raphers working in concert could hardly tran-
scribe the torrential testimony of the others.
Words flowed from them as if a monstrous res-
ervoir of words had been tapped. One could
hardly understand them, they talked so rapidly.
They were full of gestures and continually cast
their eyes toward Heaven. As a rule, they be-

longed to some obscure church or association of
believers whose exact creed regarding participation in war could not be learned. They had so
many of the ear-marks of the religious fanatic
that it was difficult to doubt their sincerity. Several of them were itinerant preachers without
pay.

One colored man had convinced me of his hon-
esty and surprised me greatly, when he had
nearly finished detailing the extent of his convictions, by saying that while he could not go to
war of his own free will, because he thought all
war was wrong, yet that he "could not help
fighting if his Government compelled him." He
would not disobey his Government, but he did
not want himself to violate his conscience. He
was quite willing, however, that the Government
should violate it for him. He was told that the
Government, under the circumstances, would expect him to fight, and he replied quite cheerfully
that he would be glad to do anything that "his
Government made him do."

Another colored objector gave the following
(a transcript from his testimony) as his reasons
for not fighting: "Because the Scriptures forbid. God told the people that when He was here,
and furthermore, besides all that, He chose two
men, one named Peter and one named Judas.
This was more than 1900 years ago and He sure-

ly knew what He was adoing. He then established the two sensibilities and they have been ruling ever since that day. Sometimes the one, which was Peter, would talk, and sometimes the other, which was Judas, would talk. * * * Well, anyway, these two sensibilities followed the people all the time and everything that happened was through the two sensibilities. The one sensibility was Peter and he was the good sensibility and the other sensibility was Judas and he was the bad sensibility. * * * Peter was the sun and Judas was the moon and they went out to tell the people that Christ will save them if they lived right and obeyed His law. So then Webster, you know Webster, he surely knew what he was talking about, * * * he said the Lord loveth His children who doeth right, so I am doing right all the time."

This man kept quoting Webster: it was "Webster said this" or "Webster said that," and obviously Webster had been a large factor in his religious life. I inquired what Webster's first name was, but he was not sure. Asked if it were Noah or Daniel, he answered, "Noah, yes sir, I guess dat is de gentleman's name." Later, when noncombatant service was suggested, he said: "No sir, I jes' can't do that. I can't take any work to kill anybody. That is jes' like shootin' a gun; no sir, I jes' can't do it. I'd

rather die right here. I am prepared to go out
of the world. I ain't made no preparation to
come into the world but I jes want to tell you,
man, that I sure am makin' big preparations to
go out.''

The colored objectors were invariably good-
natured. Their scruples as respects war were
frequently not well-reasoned, but they very
probably believed honestly the things they
claimed to believe.

### ALIENS

A surprisingly large number of the alien resi-
dents of the United States who came before the
Board, though they had for years made their
living in this country, were yet loath to fight for
it. They declared that they were ready to fight
for their native country, if returned to it, but,
without claiming any religious or other scruples,
they were unwilling to enter the war in our own
Army. Many of them were Swedes and representative of the pacifism which so long has prevailed among the Scandinavians.

Several, who had taken out their first natural-
ization papers, professed vague conscientious
scruples for the purpose of evading military
service. The sense of duty owing to the United

States possessed by the resident or by the declarant alien was negligible and lamentable. Such scruples as they professed were, for the most part, insincere, and the majority of them, upon examination, were found not to be true conscientious objectors.

### THE INTERNATIONAL BIBLE STUDENTS' ASSOCIATION

The members of this organization derived their objections to war from the rabidly pacifist writings of the late "Pastor" Charles T. Russell and from the Bible. Russell's sermons at one time were syndicated and published in four thousand newspapers and his seven books, called "Keys to the Divine Plan of the Ages", have attained a sale of over eleven million copies. The present head of the association, "Judge" J. F. Rutherford, was lately convicted of sedition.

These objectors were of all nationalities. Italians, whose testimony had to be taken through an interpreter, had read "Pastor" Russell in the Italian just as Greeks, who knew no English, had read him in the Greek. His pacifism permeates a dozen languages: the immigrant may absorb it in his native tongue before ever he comes to our shores in search of that liberty for which he will not fight.

About six per cent of the objectors examined were members of this association. Many were above the average in intelligence. Regarded as a class, they impressed one as weak characters, easily molded.

The influence of the I. B. S. A. is tremendous; it will breed more and more pacifists.

# VII

OCCASIONALLY the objectors were not informed that the Board of Inquiry was present and about to examine them; they nevertheless displayed a willingness to be questioned, whether or not they knew by whom or for what purposes the examination was to be conducted. When they were told that the Board of Inquiry was sitting, they manifested a genuine eagerness to come before it and tell their story. They appeared to welcome the visitation of ''The Board from Washington'' and in all cases that I remember they evinced no reluctance whatever to answer questions of any sort that were put to them.

They were examined without being sworn. The Mennonites and the members of kindred churches are violently opposed to the taking of an oath, and when, at times, as a test, the Board would ask, ''Do you swear to that statement?'' the reply would speedily be forthcoming, ''We do not swear, but we affirm that it is true.''

The Board functioned informally and its proceedings were simply a series of questions asked and answered. The disposition of the Board to disregard military discipline during the conduct of the examination was a matter of concern to certain of the Army officers. In one camp which I visited, a ranking officer with whom I had some acquaintance said to me, "Major, do you know that this whole camp is laughing at you?" I asked him for what reason and he said, "We are told that you allow these dirty slackers to appear before you without standing at attention and saluting. As an officer of the Army you ought to know that it is your duty to enforce discipline and to exact from your inferiors in rank the customary courtesies of the service." I informed the officer that while functioning on the Board of Inquiry my first and only duty was to determine the sincerity of objectors and that it would be contrary to the spirit of the orders were I to insist upon military observances from a class of men who strenuously insisted that they were not to be regarded as soldiers at all. The examinations were conducted in an offhand manner and without regard to any definite procedure—in every instance the Board endeavored to approach the objector in the manner which seemed best calculated to put him at his ease and thus to obtain from him the exact truth. Naturally enough, the conduct of the examinations differed very widely with different objectors.

The nomenclature of the objectors in itself is interesting—the persistence with which certain names recurred. My records show that the most frequent names were the following, or their variants: Dirksen, Thiessen, Kleinsasser, Goertz, Miller, Neufeld, Swartzendruber, Hostettler, Yoder, Entz, Unruh, Leichty, Beachy and Penner. The most usual name was Miller, with Yoder, Hostettler and Swartzendruber following closely after. The fact that these names are of German origin is probably not of significance, for nationality is not thought to be a controlling factor.

The religious objectors, although they claimed membership in a denomination opposed to war, were influenced largely by their independent reading of the Bible. To substantiate this, they quoted passages such as:

"Jesus answered, My kingdom is not of this world: if my kingdom were of this world, then would my servants fight, that I should not be delivered to the Jews." John 18.36.

"He that leadeth into captivity shall go into captivity: he that killeth with the sword must be killed with the sword." Revelation 13.10.

"Ye have heard that it was said by them of old time, Thou shalt not kill; and whosoever shall kill shall be in danger of the judgment." Matthew 5.21,

"Dearly beloved, avenge not yourselves, but rather give place unto wrath: for it is written, Vengeance is mine; I will repay, saith the Lord." Romans 12.19.

"Thou shalt not kill." Exodus 20.13.

"For the weapons of our warfare are not carnal." 2 Corinthians 10.4.

"Ye have heard that it hath been said, An eye for an eye, and a tooth for a tooth:

But I say unto you, That ye resist not evil: but whosoever shall smite thee on thy right cheek, turn to him the other also." Matthew 5.38-39.

"Ye have heard that it hath been said, Thou shalt love thy neighbour, and hate thine enemy.

But I say unto you, Love your enemies, bless them that curse you, do good to them that hate you, and pray for them which despitefully use you, and persecute you." Matthew 5.43-44.

"See that none render evil for evil unto any man; but ever follow that which is good, both among yourselves, and to all men." 1 Thessalonians 5.15.

"Thou shalt love thy neighbour as thyself." Matthew 22.39.

"Thou shalt do no murder." Matthew 19.18.

"All they that take the sword shall perish with the sword." Matthew 26.52.

It was impossible to counter these objectors by citing Matthew 10.34, Revelation 19.11, Christ and the money-changers in the Temple and other verses of similar import. Christ, they would admit, held a scourge in His hand, but nothing appears to show that He hit any one with it—probably it was for effect only upon the sheep and the oxen. The objector would sometimes attach a figurative meaning to any words which seemed, even remotely, to favor war, but would be certain to insist upon the absolute literalness of the text which he himself had chosen. He was ready to grant that certain passages appeared to contradict each other, that different persons might differently interpret the same verse, but he would not concede that the truth, as he saw it, of his own selected phrase could, for a moment, be doubted.

These men knew their Bibles. They had read in the Testaments daily, or almost daily, they testified, for a long period of years. They did not read so much for the story of it as they read it for a guide which, in all things, was to govern their conduct. They knew it narrowly, unintelligently, but they knew it. And they knew nothing else.

The unwillingness of these devout Christians to undertake works of mercy was frequently appalling. Several testified that they could work in a civilian hospital but could do nothing in a military hospital. They conceived it their Christian duty to help the wounded and the suffering, provided the wounded and the suffering were in civilian clothes, but it was to them absolutely wrong to do anything which would aid or comfort a man in uniform. Several objectors have told me that if a private soldier in camp were to be run down and severely hurt by an automobile, they would not pick the soldier up and carry him to a hospital because, the man being in uniform, such a service would be a military duty and contrary to their conscientious scruples. Nor would they, if in France, stoop down to hand a cup of water to a dying soldier because that, too, would be a military duty. It was unavailing to point out to them that Christ's sympathy was world-wide and knew no bounds; they simply could not conscientiously do anything to alleviate the suffering of a man in a uniform. The essential un-Christianity of such a class is beyond belief.

In one of the southern camps I was told, during the epidemic of influenza, that practically every one had been called upon to help in the hospitals. Nearly fifty men were dying each day. The objectors were asked to carry stretchers and otherwise to aid in saving, if possible, the lives of the stricken men. Many of the objectors refused—they could do nothing. It was against their conscience.

The small-mindedness of many of them was revealed by the unreasonable requests which they made. If an apparently sincere objector were asked if he would take a farm furlough, quite often he would inquire to what state he would be furloughed. He was told that the

Government recognized no distinction between service at home and service abroad and that he might be furloughed to a farm in this country, or he might be sent to a farm in Italy, France, England, or in any other of the allied countries. He would then say that his home was in Minnesota and he would prefer to go to some farm near his home; one man would take a farm furlough if he could be near home and could have the privilege of spending every Sunday with his wife and children. They were told that there was only one form of furlough for all men and that that was without condition or strings, and that they must take it as offered or abide by the consequences.

The matter of the uniform was often a sticking point. Many an objector expressed himself as ready to take noncombatant service except for the fact that he was required to wear the uniform. This, he said, identified him with the military establishment. One might argue with such a man for an hour, but he was unalterable—he simply could not, or would not, wear the uniform and that was all there was to it.

Not infrequently it transpired that, prior to his induction into service, an objector had been employed in some shipbuilding yard or munition plant, where he had received large

wages and where, in the shape of torpedo boats
or shrapnel, he had directly contributed toward
the war. His unwillingness to serve in the
Army was undoubtedly due to the fact that he
had been taken from a job which paid five dollars or more a day and put into service at thirty
dollars per month. If no other facts were presented this was enough to convince the Board
of the man's insincerity, and he was assigned
to service.

Many testified they had bought Liberty Bonds
or Thrift Stamps. They said that they felt it
their duty as Americans to help the Government, and they were willing to do it in this way,
because of course they did not know what the
Government would do with the money. It was
just like paying taxes—it was in no respect different, they said, than buying a three-cent, instead of a two-cent, postage stamp. In any
event, they saw nothing wrong in such pur-
chases, nor, on such explanation, did the Board.
One International Bible Student had bought
Liberty Bonds; he "knew that the buying of
Liberty Bonds was wrong" and that it was
against his conscience to buy them, but he was
compelled to purchase them in order that he
might hold his position in the Chicago bank
where he was employed. And this was taken

as a fair measure of the strength of his conscientious objections.

One objector testified that nine years ago he had immigrated to this country from Bulgaria and five years ago had taken out his first papers. He was a laborer and seemed in his wanderings to have acquired many of the characteristics of the tramp. He was of the Pentecostal faith. The Bible was the only book he read.

He said he had attended many different churches but "could not agree with them, so he went into the woods and lived as a wild man." The woods were about twenty miles south of Spokane; he built a log hut and lived in it nearly a year on fruit and nuts. He said, "I don't know why I went—God knows all. I suffered because God wanted me to. God talks to me but it is not for me to tell what he says. He says, 'I give you courage and will be by your side through to the end.' I try as far as possible to follow God and to live close to God and to seek peace with all mankind. Christ says it is wrong to fight. If you find I am not sincere in my life you can do whatever you please. I had rather obey God than man."

A singular case presented itself at Camp Lewis in the person of one Bhegat Singh. Singh was a Hindu, born in India, who had applied for citizenship and obtained his first pa-

pers. He appeared in uniform surmounted by
a huge turban. He disclaimed all idea of being
a conscientious objector and said that he was
more than anxious to help his country in the
war. He really longed to do general military
service but his religious beliefs required him
always to wear his turban; for this reason alone
he had been classified as an objector. The
Board found his objection to be conscientious
and recommended that such disposition be made
of his case as would avoid violation of his religious scruples.

So far as I have seen, there has been a slight
change in the attitude of a few objectors since
the signing of the armistice. One married objector displayed a great eagerness for a discharge. He claimed that he could do no form
of noncombatant service but could accept only
the farm furlough. When told that possibly an
abandonment of his conscientious objections
and an acceptance by him of full military service might result in his earlier discharge, he resolved to give up his objections, was found by
the Board to be insincere and assigned to general military service. Another objector had
been given a leave of absence during the Christ-
mas Holidays. He testified that he had been assured by one of his officers that his discharge
from the Army would come through a few days

after his return to camp, and, influenced by the prospect of an early discharge, he had carefully packed his Bible, which he had been so assiduously reading, had taken it home and left it there. When examined by the Board, he excused the absence of his Bible because of his forthcoming discharge.

One peculiar manifestation which I noticed was the unreadiness of the average objector to accept facts as facts, except in so far as he considered them religious facts. The things which educated men and women are willing, without personal knowledge, to take as true appear to many objectors as merely gossip which in the end may prove to have been without foundation. An example of this is found in their attitude toward the sinking of the *Lusitania*. More than one objector, when questioned about it, answered in terms such as these: "Well, that's what the papers say—I didn't see it but I might take the papers' say for it"—or, asked who sank the *Lusitania,* would answer: "Well, *the papers say* the Germans sunk it."

Many of the more intelligent class of objectors saw no harm in doing noncombatant service and in some cases evinced a real eagerness for it. They expressed themselves as desirous of doing anything which would help the country, except taking part in the actual killing or the helping to kill. Three or four objectors were examined who wore the silver chevrons (before the wearing of them had been made obligatory) as evidence that they were proud of the service which they had been permitted to perform.

# VIII

OBJECTORS may be divided roughly into three classes. We have those, first, who object to participation in war because of their membership in some church organization, the tenets of whose faith are opposed to war. Next there is the objector who, without belonging to any denomination, possesses fixed religious ideas of his own, and lastly, the objector whose objections are not religious but primarily social. These will now be considered in the order following:

## (a) THE RELIGIOUS OBJECTOR

This class, best represented by the Mennonites, views life through extremely narrow lenses. They are products of their environment and their environment is such as to throw off a pretty poor product.

As I visualize him, he lives on some isolated farm, several miles from a small country village of four or five hundred inhabitants. His parents are devout churchgoers. His family

66

has been settled here from four to six generations. He has had four or five years of schooling, probably in a church school. He attends
church regularly; the services are conducted in
German. He was taught that the Bible is the
direct word of God and he reads it almost daily.
In fact, beyond occasionally picking up a back-
country weekly newspaper, he has read nothing
besides his Bible. He does not smoke, he does
not drink, go to the theater, to moving pictures
nor attend dances. These, he thinks, are very
wrong. Probably he never has visited any
large city. He has been thrown in with people
like himself; his friends and acquaintances are
his co-religionists.

He knows nothing of what is going on in the
world. His sense of news does not extend beyond the limits of his little community. He
knows that the country is engaged in a war, but
he is ignorant of why the country entered the
war and he has small concern with it. He lives
his own petty life, and the affairs of others,
particularly those outside of his own community, do not interest him.

He was taught from his mother's knee to
pay strict obedience to the Bible, to his ministers and to his elders. His ministers and his
elders are more ingrained in the narrowness
of his sect than he and when they tell him that

war is wrong and that no Christian can fight, and he finds the same ideas in different passages in the Bible, his obsession against war becomes absolute and fixed.

One feels there is something radically wrong with this boy. He presents an ignorance which is astounding. He has no proper outlook upon anything. He is good and kind and, were he possessed of some social sense, he might in time have many of the attributes of a good citizen. His social instincts are limited to the bounds of his own neighborhood and many of these instincts—notably, his communistic ideas of property, only lately abandoned by the main body of the church and still retained by the Hutterites—are survivals from an older civilization than our own. He says he loves his country, but, inasmuch as he loves all his enemies, he has no enemies. He will not use force,. he will not fight in war, and he will take no part in fighting. He thinks the war could be won without fighting.

In many cases he is a moron. Born into the world a mental weakling, his surroundings have cramped and confined him. His ideas of non-resistance are part and parcel of his moral fiber. Stupid and dull, his mind, such as it is, is definitely made up; he assuredly believes what he says and the dictates and the forces of

government are not strong enough to tempt him
to take any chances with his immortal soul.

The Mennonites, The Brethren in Christ,
the Dunkards, the Christadelphians, the Churches of Christ, the Assemblies of God, and the
Brethren, are among the many religions, organized prior to the date of the Congressional
enactment, which are well recognized and whose
creeds forbid participation in war. The
Friends also belong to this classification but
are far more intelligent and otherwise impressed one more favorably, as has been indicated elsewhere.

The members of this class present far more
characteristics in common than do the members of either of the other classes. The Idealists and the Socialists as individuals vary greatly among themselves; the Religious Objectors,
speaking generally, are as like as two peas.

### (b) THE IDEALIST OBJECTOR

This is the second class of the religious objector. He differs from the first in that he does
not claim membership in a religious sect. He
may at one time have belonged to a denomination but, for some reason or other, he was dis-
satisfied with its teachings, became a back-
slider, and finally adopted religious views of
his own. Or he may admit retaining a passive

membership in some church, but the opinions he now so passionately urges are purely independent of it.

He differs radically from the first class in that he may have been reared in a city or in a progressive community and may be a high school or, possibly, a college graduate. His habits are correct and he is often sincerely devout in whatever religious ideas he may possess. He will sometimes say that he is a follower of Jesus in all things. His guiding principles are love, gentleness and humility.

The first class was entirely lacking in social vision; this man has entirely too much of it. His spectacles are so much the color of the rose that the frailties of human beings, and even their wars, are things to be dealt with only through gentleness and love. He is impracticable and visionary; his mentality is only half-baked. His feet long since have left the earth and his wagon is hitched to the stars.

An interesting variant of this type was found in some splendidly muscled six-footers who came from the hill districts of the southern states. They looked like football players and they turned out to be nothing but exceedingly narrow Christian idealists. They had no education, no outlook, but they were inveterate readers of the Bible, and the look of the fanatic was in their eyes. This country was not their country—they were here only temporarily as "ambassadors of Christ." The colored objector is often of this class, which comprehends very many and different types.

### (c) THE SOCIALIST OBJECTOR

Much may be overlooked in an ignoramus; much may be excused in a moron; but much, surely, can with reason be expected from a man of intelligence. The Mennonite who is not certain who General Pershing may be is deserving a certain sympathy because one feels that he is incapable of taking a decently broad view of any question; similarly, the colored man who, after working all day in a coal mine, roves about the country at night singing and preaching gratuitously to his neighbors, is very probably a fanatic and, as such, is entitled to consideration. When, however, one who has had all the advantages which birth, environment and education can give appears before you as a conscientious objector, you are bound to feel very differently about him than you may have felt about the Mennonite who preceded him, or than you will feel about the Saint in Christ (colored), who will take his place.

This man, you say, is an anomaly. The essence of his political philosophy is majority rule and yet, when the majority decides in favor of war and conscription, he becomes one of a protesting minority. He who should help, hinders and obstructs; he who should lead, by his example incites others to revolt.

He is extremely well educated, very intelligent. He perhaps attended one of the great colleges of the country and later may have taken a post-graduate course in some, perhaps a foreign, university. He has read deeply of the literature of Socialism and is glib in his utterance of its phrases.

He looks upon the United States as merely a rather pleasant place in which to live; distinctions between countries are to him artificial, arbitrary and accidental. It matters not, for instance, whether a man be American, Chinese, or German. It matters tremendously, however, whether he be a producer, or only a consumer and, so, a parasite, an exploiter. All producers comprise a brotherhood whose aims are one, whose interests interlock. Within this great proletarian brotherhood no issues are sufficient to justify combat. The producing classes must, in the end, triumph by normal, i.e., peaceful means. And so he is opposed to all and every form of warfare.

If less orthodox, he may deplore only international wars. The inter-class war, indeed, may be his ultimate objective. With no scruples against fighting as such, he rebels only against fighting in this particular war.

Or, again, he may object on what to him are philosophic, rather than economic, grounds. The State, the Army, the Church, any Institution is to him merely a name. Persons are what is real—and persons alone. The vague verbal thing called the State with its empty verbal product, the Army, are not real enough to impose any commands upon him, the Real, the Fundamental, the Person. He cannot, therefore, submit to conscription, he will not obey military orders. He will accept no arrangement proffered by Authority. He is at times the extreme absolutist.

He understands the causes of the war and is more than usually well informed about current events. He is egotistical and self-centered. He argues forcibly the cause of "Me against the Universe." He has, in part, the volubility of the colored objector and much of his fanaticism.

It is difficult to summarize the Socialist objectors because they are as different one from another as can be imagined. Many of them are simply "nuts," as they are called in the camps; some have had very little or no education; some have had too much.

This may be said in favor of the Socialist: he

commonly made an unequivocal statement of his case with no apparent concern whether his asserted scruples fell within or without the provisions of the Executive Order. Professor Gilbert Murray has written: "I think it would be true to say that the dishonest objector has had generally a better chance than the honest one. For a simple reason: that the humbug made it his whole business to please the Tribunal and get off, while the honest man did not."

The frankness of the Socialists was impressive. They appeared, in the main, to be telling the thing exactly as they saw it.

# IX

IF an objector had been found sincere and was unwilling to accept noncombatant service, several courses were open to the Board of Inquiry. If he desired it and were superior in intelligence and possessed of the necessary physique, he might be assigned to the Friends' Reconstruction Unit, subject, of course, to his acceptance by the Unit. If he were willing to accept work in the reconstruction hospitals and seemed fitted therefor, he could be placed there. Or, as was done in the larger number of cases, a farm or industrial furlough could be given to him.

To recommend a farm or industrial furlough was as far as the Board could go. The objector who expressed himself as unwilling to take it was, nevertheless, recommended for it as the Board could do nothing more for him. If, when definitely tendered the furlough by his commanding officer, he persisted in his refusal, he was then assigned to noncombatant service and became subject to all the obligations thereof.

75

If the Board recommended a man for furlough, he took it on the following conditions:

(c) that no person shall be recommended for such each person so furloughed shall be received from disinterested sources, and that the furlough may be terminated upon receipt of report that he is not working to the best of his ability; and

(b) that bona fide employment be obtained at the prevailing rate of wages for the class of work in which he engages, in the community in which he is employed.

(c) that no person shall be recommended for such furlough who does not voluntarily agree that he shall receive for his labor an amount no greater than a private's pay, plus an estimated sum for subsistence if such be not provided by the employer, and that any additional amount which may be paid for his services be contributed to the American Red Cross.''

As a rule, the farm furlough was desired by the objectors, most of whom had been farmers all their lives. The industrial furlough has been little used. The Board merely made the classification and then left the objector free to take or not to take the furlough when offered by the camp authorities.

The difficult work of administering these furloughs was entrusted to Mr. R. C. McCrea, of Columbia University, who brought to his duties a genuine fidelity of purpose, a broad sympathy and an accurate understanding of the country's

agricultural and industrial needs. So far as
was practicable the objector was placed upon a
farm where he could have freedom of worship;
preferably in a community of his co-religionists
or, in any event, in a community which was not
antagonistic to his religious beliefs. No man,
I am told, was furloughed into his home neighborhood.

Public opinion in sections of Ohio and Iowa
was counter to these furloughed objectors. The
parents and friends of drafted boys, doing service overseas or in camps, objected to the pres-
ence of these other drafted boys who, because of
their conscientious scruples, were permitted to
live and to work on comfortable farms while
their own loved ones were undergoing the rigors
of military life. Feeling ran hot, and violence
was threatened, both to the furloughed objectors and to the farmers who were employing
them. Whether or not any outbreak of consequence occurred does not appear, but it was
deemed inadvisable to furlough any more objectors into these localities.

The draft took from agriculture thousands of
young men who were sorely needed on the farms.
The farm furlough, as a measure providing an
outlet for the objectors and giving them use-
ful work, proved highly successful. The objectors were familiar with agriculture and, for the

most part, entered upon their furloughs with a real desire to do everything that they could.

A few of them, however, were contumacious and made constant and unreasonable demands upon their employers. Their food was not satisfactory, their hours of labor were too long, they were too far from their church, their work was not the sort they had in mind when they accepted the furlough, and so on, ad lib. Such complaints were investigated; if it was found that the objector was not being properly treated, the abuses complained of were promptly corrected.

In one of the western states I visited a farm to which about sixty conscientious objectors had been tentatively furloughed pending examination by the Board. The farm consists of 6500 acres and surely must be one of the model farms of this country. It is devoted wholly to the raising of corn, of which it produces about 200,000 bushels each year. I found the objectors there to be of various types, Mennonites, International Bible Students, Socialists and others.

Their services were paid for at the rate of $2.50 per day and board, out of which the objector received only $30 per month; the remainder was turned over to the American Red Cross. During corn-picking time, beginning about October 15th, their pay would be from seven to eight cents per bushel of corn picked and each man would pick about 65 bushels per day. Without the objectors it would have been impossible to harvest this crop. Certainly they proved a godsend to the farmer, and, indirectly, to the country at large. And the American Red Cross benefited substantially, as the treasury of that little country chapter would show.

The men were comfortably quartered in a large dormitory. In each room was a tin bath tub; hot and cold water were always available. The meals and the serving of the meals appeared to be entirely adequate.

The objectors were together in the mess-hall one evening and I inquired if any of them had complaints or criticisms to make of their treatment. One objector answered that he thought there should be more fly screens in the windows and the doors. I asked him if fly screens were provided for our soldiers in France and if he ought not to be willing to fight a few flies for the sake of a generous Government which had freed him from the obligation of fighting Germans. Every other objector expressed himself as satisfied with his surroundings, as indeed he might well have been.

Shortly after the armistice was signed the newspapers printed reports that objectors on furlough were to be recalled and discharged from the Army. The owner of the farm, shortly after this announcement, came to Washington, stated that most of his help had been sick with influenza, that his farm work had in consequence been greatly delayed, and that he could not possibly harvest his crop unless the objectors were allowed to remain until about the first of the year.

The report that he gave of them was most reassuring. They had, as a rule, worked faithfully and had proved very capable farmers—in fact, he had never had a better force of men on his farm. From his own observation of them, and from the reports which had come to him from his foremen, he believed that they were, in the main, sincere. He believed this, he said, in spite of the fact that some of the objectors occasionally swore at the mules; later he qualified this seeming evidence of insincerity by characterizing forcibly the average Iowa mule. Outside of the fact that some of them had taken up smoking and that one or two, upon leaving, had requested the pay which previously they had refused to accept, he saw no reason to think, after all the weeks they had spent upon his farm, that the great majority of them were other than absolutely conscientious. He was suspicious, he said, of two or three, but only suspicious.

While the examination of these objectors was

in progress, one of the Hutterite (i.e., one of the Mennonite) ministers traveled several hundred miles from his home to make a protest to the Board of Inquiry. He was perturbed to the depths by the fact that his Hutterite boys had been furloughed to a farm so far distant from their home community and church. They were missed very much; they were lonesome; they had no proper opportunity for worship where they were and it was essential that they should be furloughed to some farm nearer home where they could attend their own church and be with their own people. The good man felt so intensely about it that it seemed hard to tell him that there were hundreds of thousands of American boys in France who were even further away from their own churches and homes. This, however, made small impression upon him; he doubtless thinks to this day that the administration was most unreasonable with him and his followers.

# X

THE objectors, under the instructions, were to be segregated, and this policy was generally followed in the camps. They occupied, wherever practicable, sleeping quarters by themselves, and, wherever practicable, they had their own mess-hall. The sleeping quarters, in so far as I have observed them, were comfortable in every way and equal to the accommodations made for other drafted men. At several camps I have taken my meals in their mess-halls, and certainly no objector could conscientiously object to the meals that I have eaten there. And the meals I ate had been prepared for the objectors and were in no way different from the meals generally served to them.

The objectors who were not willing to do service of any kind spent their time in idleness or in reading their Bibles and singing hymns. They frequently held religious services. Prior to their examination by the Board, the greatest privilege was allowed to them in these respects.

and the attitude of the officers in charge seems
to have been most tolerant.

The conduct of the majority of objectors cannot seriously be criticized. They realized that
the administration had endeavored to be fair
with them, and they, in their turn, tried to be
fair with the administration. Although they refused to work they seemed desirous of avoiding
any action which would embarrass the camp authorities.

Many of the objectors evinced, on the other
hand, a disposition to hamper and to harass the
authorities in every way possible. They grum-
bled at their food; they insisted on little dainties
that no right-minded man in camp could have
demanded. They criticized the manner in which
they were segregated; they rebelled at the lack
of privileges and they complained, not only of
their beds and their bedding, but of everything
with which they came in contact. Their frame
of mind was evidenced not by words alone. Re-
bellious themselves, they sought to incite others
to rebellion. Some few planned hunger strikes
with the sole purpose of making trouble, though
it is nowhere reported that any of these strikes
was persisted in. Some few declined even to
sweep up the floor of their own quarters, to
make their own beds or to assist in the serving
of their own food. An officer in one of the west-

ern camps informed me that a group of objectors, after using the closet in the latrine, would decline to flush it on the ground that their conscience forbade.

It is not to be wondered that the officers in charge early tired of their assignments. Many a lieutenant, captain or major, eager to be on the firing line in France, was detailed to the objectors, and spent wearisome months in according fair treatment to a group of men with whom he was completely and wholly out of sympathy. No more monotonous or exacting service was rendered than that of the red-blooded Army man whose duty it was constantly to care for them. It is not surprising that, in a certain few cases, the patience of the officer was so exhausted by the maliciously annoying attitude of various objectors in his charge that he lost his temper and maltreated them. The Secretary of War, in one or two instances, ordered investigations and took disciplinary action against those responsible.

The abuse to which the objectors in camps were, on rare occasions, subjected came principally from the enlisted men. In several camps, the newly inducted soldiers who themselves were willing and anxious to fight indulged in what was intended to be a good-natured hazing but which, in several instances, resulted in a "beat-

ing up'' of the objectors. A few kicks, a bruised
arm or leg, and here and there a black eye was,
in general, all the damage done. The objector
is said to have borne his hazing well; his conscientious scruples do not appear to have been
impaired thereby.

When one considers that the country was ag-
gressively at war, that a few hundred objectors
were scattered about in a score of Army camps
and in the very midst of two million or more
fighting men, it is easily understood that here
and there ill-treatment was bound to occur. Generally, the so-called hazings were undertaken
in a spirit of fun; they very probably, on the
whole, did little harm to the objector, however
much they may have been contrary to the regulations of the Department and the discipline of
the Army. Indeed, it is to the great credit of
the Army that they were not far more common.

# XI

## "SPECIALLY QUALIFIED OFFICERS"

THE direction of the President that objectors be "placed under the command of a specially qualified officer of tact and judgment" was, in the exigencies of camp life, sometimes difficult strictly to observe. Not every man is capable of appreciating the point of view of the objector or of exercising in his dealings with him the rare degree of patience and toleration which is required. Many of the officers put in command were not of the type, mentally or temperamentally, best fitted to deal with their charges. When, however, the "specially qualified officer" was discovered, the difficulties which his camp experienced with the objectors were very greatly minimized.

I have in mind a major who was detailed to this work in a southern camp. Desirous himself of overseas service and deeply disappointed with the nature of his assignment, he yet gave to it the very best that was in him. Night and day he devoted his energies to the conscientious objector. He learned to know the men under his

care, their particular obsessions and something
of their home environment. He made it his business to be with them and to understand them,
and the record of his particular camp as regards
the objector is a brilliant one.

He succeeded in impressing the spirit of the
War Department regulations upon his men and
in making them realize that there were distinct
limitations to the Department's tolerance. His
men made little trouble and endeavored in all
ways to be obedient to the rules. His greatest
success was attained with those men who simply
thought they were conscientious objectors, or
with those whose objections were not deeply
and firmly rooted. Many who had, upon their
arrival in camp, announced themselves as objectors were, under his guidance, persuaded and
influenced to see the truth as he saw it and, in
time, to abandon their objections and take their
places in general service. Some of these men
later served overseas in the fighting forces. The
results which he was able to accomplish through
gentleness and a humane intelligence, inspirited
by a real patriotism, is ample warrant of the
value such officers have been to the administration of the Army.

The late Major General J. Franklin Bell, when
in command of Camp Upton, designated himself
as "the specially qualified officer," and took di-

rect personal charge of the objectors in his camp. Upton, perhaps because of its proximity to large cities, had more than its share of Socialists.

General Bell himself read and explained the Executive Order to his objectors. Both the Order and his own interpretation of it he caused to be printed and circulated among them. He spent much time and energy with his objectors and, as a result, many of them, including not a few Socialists, were induced to take up combatant service.

### XII

### THE INSINCERE OBJECTOR

THE objector determined by the Board to be insincere does not, as a rule, differ in outward appearance from the sincere objector. He is apt to be quite as honest-looking and to be quite as obdurate in asserting his opinions.

His insincerity manifests itself commonly in some missing or faulty link in his chain of evidence. He admits, generally without reluctance, some act patently inconsistent with his avowed position. The instance of the objector who bought bonds under compulsion or of the one who was eager to take up his old work in a munition factory or a Government shipyard is pertinent.

Family concerns were frequently the source of what the objector asserted to be scruples against warfare. A fairly religious type of man who had a sick wife or a family which could ill be supported by his pay and allowances would worry so constantly about domestic affairs that often, in seeking excuses for a discharge from the Army, he would amplify and extend his religious ideas so that they would approximate, to his own mind, conscientious scruples.

A member of the "Church of God and Christ", as my record shows it, testified that he was twenty-eight years old, that he had led a more or less irregular life without religion until, in May, 1918, he had "consecrated himself to the church." He presented, however, no evidences of having pondered much upon a future life nor of possessing even a fair acquaintance with the Bible. When pressed as to the determining factor which had so lately induced him to join a church he said: "I was married last June. I couldn't get married unless I belonged to the church. My woman belonged and wouldn't have me unless I joined the church." After having "entered the fold" for the sake of a woman rather than for the sake of his God, he evaded participation in war, not because he thought war was wrong, but merely because he was reluctant to leave his wife.

A peculiar state of facts was presented by another objector. He had some pretentions to culture and had acquired a hodge-podge of an education, having drifted about from one college to another. Inconsistency was part and parcel of him. Originally, he had belonged to one of the old established churches in which he and his family had been brought up. He had attended this church regularly up to the time of his entrance into college, when he conceived the notion that his social position would be better if he belonged to some other denomination.

He fumbled about, experimenting first with one religion and then another, seeking that which in the end should give him the best social standing. When he was before the Board, his religious ideas were still in a state of flux—he did not know what he believed nor where he belonged.

Upon being closely questioned in an effort to determine his exact ethical whereabouts, he broke into tears and admitted that the only reason for his seeking a release from the Army was the old mother who was dependent on him for support; and that he really had no fixed conscientious scruples at all. He confessed that he was afraid to go to war. He was assigned, as insincere, to general service; later, representations were made to the Board that he had a bad mental history and his case was granted a rehearing.

"The Camp Dodger", a newspaper published by the men at Camp Dodge, Iowa, contained in its issue of January 4, 1919, the following:

"His religion, which would not permit him to wear the uniform of a soldier, went back on Priv. Joshua A. Hoffer, Bridgewater, S. D., when he was discharged from the Army last week.

"Hoffer, who is a Mennonite and maintained that he was a conscientious objector to military service, refused to wear the uniform after he was inducted. No arguments could batter down his religious scruples on this score and all the time he was in the service he wore his civilian clothing and was assigned to noncombatant duties.

"Evidently Hoffer admired the men around him who wore the uniform, and when he was discharged he hied himself to Dodge City and purchased a classy uniform to show the folks at home how he looked as a 'soldier.' His religion gave way to pride in his personal appearance and his conscientious scruples gave way to his vanity.''

A few days after the foregoing was published I inquired about it at Camp Dodge and was assured by different officers that it actually had happened.

The glamor of the uniform irresistibly made its appeal to some of the objectors. Several appeared before the Board wearing wrist watches. They were careful, however, to explain that the watches had been given to them by their "folks"; that they were worn simply because of convenience and despite their association with the uniform. Several who testified that the uniform had been "forced upon them" had, nevertheless, had their pictures taken in it and sent home to admiring friends and relatives.

# XIII

THESE men, who have been called "the logicians of conscience, the extremists of peace," have been the objectors most difficult to contend with. They are so conscientious that they will do nothing; they will not fight, they will not do noncombatant service, they will not take a farm or industrial furlough. They utterly refuse to submit to conscription; they will play no part in the military establishment.

One of them who claimed to be desirous of service in the Friends' Reconstruction Unit was offered such service by the Board. He refused it—he would not consider it unless he were first discharged from the Army. To accept a designation to it by the Board would be an acknowledgment that the Government had power to draft him—this he would never admit. But, once free of the Army, he would yearn for such service! The distaste for conscription was even stronger to this enlightened gentleman than his craving to alleviate human suffering.

Many of this class are unquestionably sincere. What, however, is their sincerity worth?

They have been a burden in a time of world crisis. They have contributed nothing save discontent and disaffection. They come out from the war resolved to spread the gospel of their own iniquity.

They are direct beneficiaries of all that the allied armies have accomplished. The titles to their farms and homes have been validated by the men who fought in the trenches of France. They share in all the fruits of the war and they object to none of the blessings of the victory.

The parody of Goldsmith's poem "The Hermit", quoted by Bishop Cooke, is directly applicable:

> "No flocks that roam the valley free,
>     To slaughter I condemn;
> The butchers kill the meat for me;
>     I buy the meat of them."

# XIV

## PROPAGANDA AMONG OBJECTORS

ALMOST every religious objector had in his possession a well-worn Bible or New Testament, in the fly-leaves of which he had written out his favorite scriptural quotations. Usually these quotations had been selected by the objector himself, although various religious denominations printed and circulated among their adherents pamphlets which contained verses bearing directly upon non-participation in war. Many of these were printed in German.

Copies of the instructions issued by the Secretary of War were widely current among objectors, who received them in some cases before even the Commanding General of the camp had been apprized of their existence. In one camp which I visited an objector called attention to a certain War Department ruling days before it was given out to the Board of Inquiry. Somewhere, surely, there were leaks.

An officer told me that some of the objectors were regular subscribers to a press-clipping bureau which kept them supplied with every item of news bearing upon objectors and the War Department. They received frequent visits from the pastors and leaders of their churches and few of these visits were prompted by anything other than a desire to stiffen the objector in his resolution not to participate in war. Here and there, however, a preacher of the Seventh Day Adventist Church desired to impress upon his objectors their duty to serve in some noncombatant capacity.

"Trench and Camp", a weekly printed at Fort Oglethorpe, Georgia, in its issue of September 23, 1918, reported that the Mennonites at Camp Greenleaf had addressed a letter to President Mosiman of Bluffton College, a Mennonite institution in Bluffton, Ohio, in which they asked certain questions regarding work in the Army which they as Mennonites could properly perform.

From President Mosiman's reply, as given in "Trench and Camp", the following extracts are taken:

"It is impossible for me to tell you what to do. This is a matter of conscience and it is your conscience that must decide and not mine. I fear that many of our boys have only got themselves into trouble by much well-meant advice. * * *"

"Personally, I feel that in this time of war every citizen owes his country some service. I feel that it is up to the conscientious objector to do more in the service that he undertakes than the average soldier. I might add that almost all the boys that have gone out from Bluffton College are in the hospital service. My advice to them was that they should prove themselves worthy of their country. They have, on the whole, received splendid treatment and have done good work in the hospital. Of course, I cannot say that you shall do the same, if your conscience does not permit. * * * No Mennonite has a right to exemption as a Mennonite, but only as a conscientious objector. * * *''

''I hate war as much as any one. But I have seen the menace of German militarism from two and a half years' residence in Germany, and I have trembled when I saw it. I have exclaimed, 'What will happen if the Beast should ever break loose?' America did not want this war. The Mennonites who came to this country to escape war, because they hated it, wanted it least of all. Not to fight has been bred into us. But not that we should not love our country. * * * So there can be no thought in the choice of service that would take us away from danger. Nor should there be hair-splitting about wearing the uniform and such things.''

The admirable tone of this letter seems to have been little heeded by the Mennonites.

Evidence of propaganda was found in the phrases, taken mainly from Departmental orders, which constantly recurred in the testimony of the objectors. The Mennonite who could ill express himself in English made an easy mouthful of such phrases as ''military establishment,'' ''participation in war,'' ''conscientious scruples,'' and ''religious convictions.'' He could not, at first sight, have read any of the orders had they been printed in words of one syllable. Obviously, they had been read over and explained to him and he had been taught, parrot-like, to recognize and to repeat the words upon which, it was thought, his status so largely would depend.

Mr. Rhodes in his "History of the United States", is authority for the following reference to Civil War days: "From a resolution of the House it appeared that some dissatisfaction was caused by the exemption of certain preachers and not of others; and word came from Harrisburg of the 'rapid increase in Pennsylvania of noncombatant sects. The Quakers, Dunkards and Mennonites,' it was added, 'are having more than a revival.'"

The "Herold der Wahrheit", an organ of the Old Amish Mennonites, published at Scottdale, Pennsylvania, featured its "Correspondence from Furloughed Brethren" from which are taken parts of a letter from one who signs himself, "A humble brother, Abraham Weaver":

"* * * This week I received a letter from a brother in camp, who is spending dark and dreary days, like many have experienced in the past year, but still we can be thankful that God was so merciful, and brought something to draw His people nearer to Him again, and strengthen the churches spiritually, but such times are not joyful. * * *

"It is said that spinal meningitis is starting in some camps. * * *

"I have spent ten months in the camp (God only knows how much longer I have to spend there) ; never before could I realize how dear home was, and how pleasant it was to be at home with parents, until I had to depart. * * *

"I received a letter from Aaron Loucks a few days ago, and the chances are, that I have to go to camp again when my furlough expires, which is Nov. 15, but I would be glad to receive the 'Herold' wherever I may be. It may be possible that I can stay where I am at present, as I hope I can."

The Reverend Aaron Loucks of Scottdale, Pa., was constantly busy in advising his Mennonite followers regarding their rights. He exerted a pernicious influence and was persuaded to discontinue his propaganda only when the War Department threatened him with the Espionage Law.

Organized societies made it their business to furnish to objectors or to potential objectors the rulings of the War Department and circulated pamphlets designed solely to create opposition to the Selective Service Law.

# XV

## THE ATTITUDE OF THE WAR DEPARTMENT

The instructions relating to conscientious objectors were issued in the name of the Secretary of War, who at all times took an active interest in formulating a course which was intended to be fair to the objector and just to the country at large. The direct administration of the objectors was delegated to the Third Assistant Secretary of War, Mr. F. P. Keppel.

The writer has twice discussed questions relating to objectors with Secretary Baker, and very many times with Secretary Keppel. I have found them equally prompt to remedy an injustice to an objector as to correct an injustice to the fighting man. The War Department, actuated by the spirit of the Executive Order, had framed regulations which it insisted should be strictly observed, not only by the officers in command, but by the objectors themselves. Secretary Baker and Secretary Keppel have as often construed the regulations against the objector as they have construed them in his favor.

# XVI

THERE has prevailed so widespread a criticism of the policy of exempting objectors, in part or in whole, from military service, that it is surprising that some of the critics have not dipped more deeply into their state constitutions. For example, the constitution of the state of Colorado contains the following, in section 5, Article 17:

"No person having conscientious scruples against bearing arms shall be compelled to do militia duty in times of peace: provided, such person shall pay an equivalent for such exemption."

The constitution of the state of Indiana, in section 6, Article 12, reads thus:

"No person conscientiously opposed to bearing arms shall be compelled to do militia duty; but such person shall pay an equivalent for exemption; the amount to be prescribed by law."

More or less similar provisions are found in the constitutions of Idaho, Illinois, Iowa, Kansas, Kentucky, Louisiana, Maine, Michigan,

Missouri, New Hampshire, North Carolina,
North Dakota, Oregon, Pennsylvania, South
Carolina, South Dakota, Tennessee, Washing-
ton and Wyoming.

## XVII

I HAVE never visited a disciplinary barracks and so know nothing at first hand of the treatment there accorded to the military prisoners. At Camp Dodge I examined a dozen or more men who had served terms of from three weeks to four months in the Disciplinary Barracks at Leavenworth. I inquired closely into their treatment and every one asserted that he "couldn't complain of the manner in which he had been used." Some told me that they had *heard* of others who had not fared so well but no one of the dozen had anything to say except that he had been "fairly treated" or "treated as well as a prisoner could expect." Nothing appears from the testimony of these objectors which justifies criticism of the officials at Leavenworth.

The Board of Inquiry was formed for the purpose of examining objectors at cantonments, as soon as possible after their induction into service. It had nothing to do officially with those objectors who, through disobedience of orders or other misconduct, had been tried and sentenced by courts-martial. Such men became general prisoners and therefore not within the jurisdiction of the Board.

The men I saw at Dodge had been released from custody and restored to their former status as objectors. They had not previously been before the Board and clearly were entitled to a hearing.

# XVIII

In spite of the fact that the objector's name and ancestry are most often German, it is not believed that the objectors, as a class, are pro-German. The greater number by far of them are native-born citizens whose national sympathies (so far as they have any at all) are with America.

I doubt, too, if alien parentage or foreign birth often has a direct connection with their refusal to participate in war. Most of the objectors are Mennonites, and their unwillingness openly to state their adherence as between Germany and the United States proceeds from their belief that "it is not for me to judge."

The psychological report of the Surgeon General shows that of 720 cases examined in Camps Sherman, Pike, Kearney, Bowie, Meade, Upton and Lee, ninety per cent are native born and ten per cent foreign born; approximately one third are of American parentage, one third German and one third Russian, English, Scotch, Irish and Scandinavian.

105

# XIX

## THE OBJECTOR IN PEACE TIMES

THE objector, although a manifestation of war, is essentially a product of peace. The occasion for his objecting is war; the cause of his objecting has been long existent in his environment and heredity.

Since April 6, 1917, the country has been most alert in watching the enemy alien, the German propagandist and the objector. Presumably, with the coming of peace our observation of them will end. We ought, however, to keep the objector in mind and to remember that peace, which gave him birth, will continue to breed more like him.

Something must be done to uplift and to nationalize the backward people who need so sorely the broadening effects of education. Something, as well, must be done to check the immigration of those aliens who bring to our shores their strange and un-American beliefs.

The Government, or some body of citizens, carefully should scrutinize the conduct of those objectors who have been and who will be discharged from the Army, and observe if the same degree of conscientious exactitude prevails among them in their home communities as they manifested during their sojourn in the camps.

The objector, in all truth, constitutes a minor problem. No one can be certain, however, that in the event of another war his problem may not be far more bothersome. He should by no means be neglected because peace has come; rather our interest in him should now be intensified.

# XX

THE story of Richard L. Stierheim reads like a page of romance. Stierheim, although an objector, had probably never received the offer of noncombatant service provided for by the Executive Order; on the other hand, it seemingly nowhere appears that he had advised his commanding officer that he claimed to be an objector. He was sent overseas in Company D, 315th Infantry. Finding himself in a combatant unit and his company about to go into action against the enemy, he left his organization and remained absent until apprehended on the Spanish border some days later.

When tried by court-martial for his desertion he testified that he had left his company because he didn't believe in war. He said: ''By going up to the front and being killed I didn't see how I could stand up on Judgment Day and say I died fighting for God Almighty.'' He admitted that his object in deserting was to avoid the necessity of going into battle.

The following facts are shown by letters from his Commanding General and others:

"On the night of November 3, 1918, during an attack of his company and organization against Hill 378, north of Verdun, Stierheim volunteered to go out into 'No-Man's Land' at night to rescue wounded men. He rescued six wounded men unassisted, while a great number of machine guns were firing at him. One wounded man who had been shot six times was behind a tree from which he could not move; Stierheim walked over and brought him in. After his company had been relieved and was in the rear under cover from shell fire, he volunteered to go forward again with the regimental chaplain to help bury the dead. Thereafter he volunteered to be one of a litter party to carry wounded to a Battalion Aid Post, maintained by Captain Bulford in a dugout in a valley below a farm house; and thence to the Regimental Aid Post. This valley was under considerable shell fire during most of the time, and it was often quite difficult to get patients to the Aid Post, and also to evacuate them to the Regimental Post, because of the shell fire, and also because of mud, shell holes and steep grades; but during the following eight or nine days, and until the declaration of the armistice on November 11, 1918, Stierheim conducted many patients through the valley, and showed an absolute indifference to danger. He also made many trips to the farm house for water for the wounded men, under heavy fire."

Lieutenant Gallagher, his company commander, in writing of Stierheim's conduct, says: "I have never seen such bravery, and feel that a man of his caliber deserves some consideration," and recommends clemency "for his conspicuous gallantry, unselfish and untiring efforts."

Captain Bulford writes of him: "This man showed courage and devotion to duty far above the average and it is desired that the Commanding Officer be informed of his courageous work."

Stierheim deserved "some consideration" and he got it. General Pershing, Commander-in-Chief of the American Expeditionary Forces, forwarded the record of Steirheim's trial to the Judge Advocate General with this statement:

"I have not confirmed the sentence because, while the evidence clearly shows that the accused was guilty of desertion as charged, and the sentence was therefore warranted, his subsequent voluntary and meritorious service in action, as more particularly referred to in the above mentioned letter of the Commanding General of the 79th Division, and the recommendation of the accused's company commander, prompt me to recommend that the entire sentence be remitted, and that he be restored to duty and assigned to noncombatant service. With this recommendation I transmit the record for the action of the President."

# XXI

THE plan adopted by our Government during the war does not differ in essential aspects from the plan adopted by Great Britain. Many of their features were taken from the law passed during the Civil War, and some details have persisted since the days of Napoleon, since the days of the Roman Empire. It cannot be asserted, however, that under any known scheme has absolute justice been done either to the objectors or to the fighting men.

Colonel Roosevelt, as may be expected, entertained radical ideas regarding objectors. In an article in the "Kansas City Star" he wrote as follows:

"No man has any right to remain in a free country like ours if he refuses, whether conscientiously or unconscientiously, to do the duties of peace and of war which are necessary if it is to be kept free. The true lovers of peace recognize their duty to fight for freedom. The Society of Friends has furnished the same large proportion of soldiers for this war that it did for the Civil War.

"It is all wrong to permit conscientious objectors to

111

remain in camp or military posts or to go back to their homes. They should be treated in one of three ways: First, demand of them military service, except the actual use of weapons with intent to kill, and if they refuse to render this service treat them as criminals and imprison them at hard labor; second, put them in labor battalions and send them to France behind the lines, where association with soldiers might have a missionary effect on them and cause them to forget their present base creed and rise to worthy levels in an atmosphere of self-sacrifice and of service and struggle for great ideals; third, if both of the above procedures are regarded as too drastic, intern them with alien enemies and send them permanently out of the country as soon as possible.''

A goodly portion of the more intelligent objectors will probably always be willing to accept noncombatant service. It is well to encourage such men to enter this service, but it seems rather hopeless to treat as criminals those who refuse. Some outlet surely should be found for the sincere objector who is conscientiously opposed to noncombatant service.

Little fault can be found with the second suggestion, for those men who are willing to serve in labor battalions at all are not unwilling, as a rule, so to serve behind the lines. In fact, the majority of those who were offered the farm furlough were quite willing to take it in any part of the world to which they might be detailed.

There remain, however, the so-called absolutists—that is, those men who are unwilling to do any service whatsoever in the Army or under conscription. Deportation for these men seems none too severe.

If the war had continued longer, many furloughed objectors would have been sent overseas to do farm or other labor. In fact, the Department had already approved this plan when the armistice intervened. The shipping abroad of a considerable number of them would probably have had a deterrent effect upon the weaker objectors at home and, possibly, for the reasons suggested by Colonel Roosevelt, might have had a wholesome influence upon the men themselves. Experience in the camps at home has not, however, justified the latter assumption.

It is not fair to the fighting man who stands ready, subject to orders, to go to Siberia, Italy, or to the firing line in France, that an objector, simply because he has been found honest, should be assured an absolutely safe abiding place on an American farm. So long as the objector's scruples are respected, there is no reason why he should not run the same risks of ocean travel, at any rate, as are endured by his fighting brother.

The segregation recommended by the Executive Order possesses obvious disadvantages. It tends irresistibly to develop an *esprit de corps* among the objectors; it furnishes the best possible opportunity for propaganda and for different groups of objectors to discuss sympathetically their points of opposition to warfare and thus to bolster up the spirits of those who are inclined to wobble. Granting that segregation possesses all these defects, it yet seems a far preferable policy to that of concentrating the objectors among the combatant units.

Segregation would be much better, however, if the objectors were actually segregated, i. e., by themselves, absolutely apart from the fighting men. If, instead of having a colony of a hundred or more objectors quartered in a military camp, where every other drafted man could see them lolling about and basking in the sun, they were to be kept in a place miles away from any other soldiers, their very isolation would then be productive of much of the good which segregation now absolutely misses.

If the quartering of all the objectors in a single place were to impose too great a burden upon the Department, three or four convenient posts could be found in various parts of the country where they could be cared for entirely separate and distinct from any body of real soldiers.

It would undoubtedly be advisable if, in future, the British system of determining their sincerity by local boards were to be adopted. A Board composed of three members, designed to function over the whole United States, is far too small. The trial of sincerity might well be had before ever the objector reports to camp. There should be opportunity not only for a greater degree of proof, but the Government should insist that the tenets of a given church as regards warfare should be evidenced by the testimony of the leading men of that church, as well as by its articles of faith. The membership claimed by the objector should be supported by independent witnesses. His conduct, his character, his adherence to his creed, should be made the subject of competent proof.

The individual objector should likewise be most closely scrutinized; his statements, wherever possible, should be supported by outside testimony. The sincerity of each objector should, with as much detail and with as great a particularity, be tried and tested as matters of fact are commonly tried and tested in a court of law. The objector should be sworn or affirmed; the proceedings should be transcribed by a court reporter and preserved as public records.

The Government should now proceed definitely to determine upon a plan of action with respect to objectors. It should weigh the question carefully and strive equally to do justice to the objector and to avoid injustice to the patriotic citizen. Once it decides upon a proper policy, it should enact that policy into positive law.

There has been a general feeling among objectors that the Government, in the end, would be lenient with them. If they had been sentenced by a court-martial to a term of imprisonment, the impression prevailed that sooner or later they would all be pardoned. In other words, many of the sentences were not taken seriously.

The enactment of a statute dealing broadly with the subject would, in the event of another war, resolve all doubts as to the status of the objector. He would know exactly where he stood; that the nation had soberly made up its mind.

I have attempted in these pages to summarize some of my experiences with objectors in the hope that a better understanding of the problem may result. If what I have set down here should prove of some small value in directing attention to the more important aspects of the subject, the purpose of this book will amply be achieved.

I have these things to suggest:

First: that the sincerity of all men presenting themselves as objectors be tried and determined. The insincere objectors should be put into general military service.

Second: that the sincere objectors who are willing to accept noncombatant service should be assigned to noncombatant service.

Third: that the sincere objectors who are unwilling to take noncombatant service should be given farm or industrial furloughs.

Fourth: that the objectors who are unwilling to take either noncombatant service or farm or industrial furloughs should be deported from the United States of America.

Fifth: if deportation is not possible because of the refusal of other countries to receive these absolutists, or for other reasons, then the United States must harbor them. Inasmuch as they have no right to a voice in governmental affairs, they should be disfranchised.

Great Britain has introduced a bill to deprive an objector of his vote for a period of years. Canada already has enacted: ''All persons who shall have voted at a Dominion election held subsequent to the 7th day of October, 1917 * * * shall be ineligible and incompetent (a) to apply for, or to be granted * * * exemption from combatant military or naval service on conscientious grounds, or (b) to be excepted as a Mennonite or as a Doukhobor * * * or exempted as such from combatant * * * service on conscientious grounds." (The Dominion Election Act, Chapter 6, s. 67.) A full measure of citizenship should assuredly not be accorded to the absolutists.

It has been suggested that they be colonized in some remote place where they could talk and argue to their heart's content—but by themselves. There, as absolutists, as citizens of the World but of no country, they would be free to live their lives, subject only to the restrictions which a sovereign government, mindful of her honor, must needfully impose.

The practical difficulties of this plan immediately suggest themselves. Something, however, should be done, to make definite and certain the standing of such men if ever again the Government should call upon the manhood of the states.

# XXII

## (a) *For*

THE arguments in favor of the objector take different forms and they may thus be summarized: Conscience, the God-given "stop in the mind", as old John Woolman called it, should be inviolable. No man should be forced to disregard the will of his Creator, as that will is revealed to him.

"To the sincerely religious person Conscience," writes Mr. Sidney Webb, "is the direct message of God to the individual—not in the earthquake or the thunder—not even in argument or in ratiocination—but in the still small voice is the divine instruction to be found; and when it is found its authority is supreme. It is above conventional morality, above the law of the State * * *"

Or, as "The New Republic" puts it: "No free state can possibly make a crime out of refusal to serve in war when such refusal is actuated by sincere conscientious motives. We may consider such an attitude illogical, absurd. We

119

may see grave public inconveniences in it. But we have passed beyond the point of barbarism in which men presume to distinguish between the logical and the illogical, the serviceable and the disserviceable in other men's consciences. We do not compel men to eat meat on Friday if their consciences require them to fast. We do not require men to eat swine's flesh when their consciences pronounce it an abomination. And if a man's conscience forbids him to serve in war, or to perform any service that even indirectly bears upon war, we are bound to respect it. To attempt by threats and penalties to force such a man into military service would be tyranny as hideous as that of the Roman proconsul who slew the seven brothers and their mother because they refused to eat swine's flesh."

"The Survey" for December 7, 1918, quotes the author of an English book entitled "Prisoners of Hope" as follows: " 'When, then, I am told that the conscientious objector in refusing to defend his country is declining to discharge a fundamental duty, I cannot admit the justice of the accusation. His first duty is not to himself, his family, his municipality, his country or to humanity. His first duty is to God. When, after seeking by the best means in his power, to enlighten his mind and liberate his judgment, he has reached the conviction that armed resistance is contrary to the will of God, he is bound to accept it at whatever cost. * * * Our city is dear to us, our Country dearer still, humanity dearer than either. But here we have no abiding city, for our true home is in the eternal and the unseen. From the swift procession of unstable empires we look for the city which hath foundations, whose Builder and Maker is God. * * * We know of a loftier patriotism than the love of our native land or the deeper love which embraces all mankind. Our heart thrills to the challenge of Marcus Aurelius: ''He says, 'Dear city of Cecrops'; wilt thou not say 'Dear City of God?' '' Indeed for multitudes of us it is this higher patriotism which inspires and sustains the lower.' ''

## (b) *Against*

''It is even more easy to pretend to a conscientious objection than it is to pretend to sciatica,'' says Mr. Sidney Webb in his illuminating discussion of the subject in ''The North American Review.''

Conscience is so intimate and personal a thing that the question whether or not it is present in a controlling degree must of necessity be determined by the objector alone. He must, perforce, judge his own case.

The notion that the dictates of conscience should constitute a defense to the commission of a crime is repugnant to all systems of justice. No judge would, for a moment, listen to a burglar who had broken into a house solely because he conscientiously believed that he needed his neighbor's bread, nor to a self-confessed murderer who should say that he had killed his friend because he had been driven by a conscientious conviction that the friend had to be killed. Conscience which, as a plea, is not heeded in a court of law should carry no more weight when urged as an excuse from war.

We who have chosen to live under our government must abide by its laws. When the nation, impelled by sorest necessity, resolves to take up arms against a foe, it is our duty, as citizens all, to obey the national will and fight for the maintenance of the institutions under which we have lived.

Professor A. V. Dicey finely says in an article in "The Nineteenth Century and After" for February, 1918: "The pity naturally and in some respects rightly felt for the objector, because he is looked upon as a man suffering for conscience' sake, is obscuring the facts that the objector's conscience misguides him, and that some Englishmen are in danger of forgetting that the thousands of men of whose deaths we

daily hear, and also the thousands of men of
whose deaths we do not hear at all, are each
obeying the dictates of his conscience, and of a
conscience none the less enlightened because it
stimulates manifest self-sacrifice and is guided
by the love of England.

"The scrupulosity in short of the objector
is entitled to no more respect than the conscience of the obedient soldier, and the moment
has arrived when, even though wishing to deal
justly with the heart-searchings of the impris-
oned objector, we must remember that such a
man comes into conflict, not with an Act of Par-
liament passed to-day or yesterday, but with a
moral law of natural patriotism which has been
established for ages, has been the protection of
human liberty, and is the necessary condition of
human progress.   This must be borne in mind.
All that it is here however necessary to maintain is that there are more reasons than some
most excellent Englishmen now understand for
holding that submission to the law of the land
is in the vast majority of cases the personal
duty of every loyal citizen. * * * The vast majority of British citizens are convinced that,
when England and the British Empire are engaged in a life and death struggle on behalf of
national freedom and independence, the crotch-
ets, the scruples, the tenderness of the indi-

vidual conscience must yield to the necessity of preserving the life and the liberty of England.''

The case against the objector cannot in justice be left without quoting from an earlier writer (not without an indwelling ''daemon'' himself) who assumes The Laws to be speaking to him in this wise:

''Tell us: What complaints have you to make against us which justify you in attempting to destroy us and the State? In the first place, did we not bring you into existence? Your father married your mother by our aid and begat you. Say whether you have any objection to urge against those of us who regulate marriage?'' None, I should reply. ''Or against those of us who after birth regulate the nurture and education of children in which you also were trained? Were not the laws, which have the charge of education, right in commanding your father to train you in music and gymnastics?'' Right, I should reply. ''Well then, since you were brought into the world and nurtured and educated by us, can you deny in the first place that you are our child and servant, as your fathers were before you? Would you have a right to strike or revile or do any other evil to your father or your master, if you had one, because you have been struck or reviled by him, or received some other evil at his hands? You

would not say this? And because they think
right to destroy you, do you think that you have
any right to destroy us in return, and your country, as far as in you lies? Will you, O professor of true virtue, pretend that you are justified in this? Has a philosopher like you failed
to discover that our country is more to be
valued and higher and holier far than mother or
father, or any ancestor, and more to be respected in the eyes of the gods and of men of
understanding? Also to be soothed, and gently
and reverently entreated when angry, even
more than a father, and either to be persuaded,
or if not persuaded to be obeyed? And when
we are punished by her, whether with imprisonment or stripes, the punishment is to be endured
in silence; and if she leads us to wounds or
death in battle, thither we follow as is right;
neither may any one yield or retreat or leave
his rank, but whether in battle or in a court of
law, or any other place, he must do what his
city and his country order him; or he must
change their view of what is just; and if he may
do no violence to his father or mother, much less
may he do violence to his country." What answer shall we make to this, Crito? Do the laws
speak truly, or do they not?

*Crito:* I think that they do.

*Socrates:* Then The Laws will say: "Consider, Socrates, if this is true, that in your present attempt you are going to do us wrong.  For after having brought you into the world, and nurtured and educated you, and given you and every other citizen a share in every good that we had to give, we further proclaim and give the right to every Athenian, that if he does not like us when he has come of age and has seen the ways of the city, and made our acquaintance, he may go where he pleases and take his goods with him; and none of us laws will forbid him or interfere with him.  Any of you who does not like us and the city, and who wants to go to a colony or to any other city, may go where he likes, and take his goods with him.  But he who has experience of the manner in which we order justice and administer the State, and still remains, has entered into an implied contract that he will do as we command him.''

## APPENDICES

### I.

The Adjutant General's Office, as of December 24, 1918, reported "from available records and by estimation," the approximate number of objectors examined by the Board of Inquiry as:

| | |
|---|---:|
| Recommended for farm or industrial furlough | 1,500 |
| Recommended for Friends' Reconstruction Unit | 88 |
| Recommended for noncombatant service | 390 |
| Assigned to general military service (insincere) | 122 |
| | 2,100 |

The above figures do not include the objectors, estimated at about 1,300, who accepted noncombatant service and were assigned thereto without examination by the Board; nor those, estimated to be about 400, who were, at the date named, general prisoners at Leavenworth."

The total number of men in the Army, accepted or recognized as conscientious objectors, was about 3,900.

### II.

This table, compiled from figures furnished by The Adjutant General's Office as of December 20, 1918, shows the principal classifications of objectors made by the Board of Inquiry:

| Class 1-A & 1-B | 1-C | 2-A | 2-B | 2-C | 3 |
|---|---|---|---|---|---|
| 1,500 ...... | 88 | 219 | 156 | 15 | 122 |

For meaning of classifications, see pages 37-38.

## III

The table following shows the number of organizations and the membership thereof of certain denominations heretofore mentioned. It is taken, in large part, from the publication entitled, "Religious Bodies: 1906," and supplements thereto, issued by the Bureau of Census:

| DENOMINATION | ORGANI-ZATIONS | MEMBERS |
|---|---|---|
| Adventists (5 bodies) ......... | 2,668 | 114,915 |
| Brethren (Dunkards) .......... | 1,287 | 133,626 |
| Christadelphians .............. | 70 | 1,412 |
| Church of God and Saints in Christ (colored) ........... | 48 | 1,823 |
| Churches of the Living God (colored) ..................... | 67 | 4,276 |
| Friends ...................... | 1,027 | 112,982 |
| Mennonites (16 bodies).......... | 838 | 79,363 |
| Pentecostal Church of the Nazarene ...................... | 100 | 6,657 |
| Churches of Christ............. | 5,570 | 317,937 |

## IV

Table showing "the religious denominations of 1,060 conscientious objectors" in twelve camps:

| | |
|---|---|
| Mennonites ....................... | 554 |
| Friends ......................... | 80 |
| International Bible Students......... | 60 |
| Dunkards ....................... | 37 |
| Israelites of the House of David...... | 39 |

| | |
|---|---|
| Church of Christ | 31 |
| Church of God, etc. (colored) | 20 |
| Seventh Day Adventists | 20 |
| Pentecostal Assembly | 13 |
| All other denominations | 206 |

"More than one-half of the conscientious objectors are Mennonites of one branch or another. The Quakers, Brethren, Dunkards, International Bible Students Association (Russellites) and Israelites of the House of David constitute about 25 per cent of the whole. These, taken with the Mennonites, make up fully 75 per cent of the conscientious objector body."

The foregoing table together with Tables V and VI are excerpts from a report, compiled by Lieutenant Mark A. May, made by the Division of Psychology, Surgeon General's Office, U. S. A.

## V

Table showing "the percentage of 880 objectors who reached various grades in school:

| GRADE REACHED | PER CENT |
|---|---|
| 0 | 100 |
| 1 | 99 |
| 2 | 98 |
| 3 | 97 |
| 4 | 94 |
| 5 | 88 |
| 6 | 80 |
| 7 | 70 |
| 8 | 58 |
| High School, first year | 42 |
| " " second year | 29 |
| " " third year | 24 |
| " " fourth year | 18 |
| College, first year | 12 |
| " second year | 9 |

GRADE REACHED          PER CENT

| | |
|---|---|
| College, third year | 6 |
| "     fourth year | 3 |

Less than 10 per cent of the Mennonites went beyond the 8th grade. The 12 per cent who reached college are, as far as the data show, either Socialists, Dunkards or Friends, with a few I. B. S. A. (Russellites)."

## VI

Table showing the specific objections of about 500 cases in Camps Custer, Grant, Greenleaf, Pike and Sherman:

| | |
|---|---|
| War is forbidden by church and creed | 115 |
| "    "    "    in the Scriptures in general | 125 |
| "    "    "    by Christ specifically | 95 |
| "    "    "    by the Commandment | 60 |
| "    "    "    by conscience | 120 |
| " promotes evil | 16 |
| " is wrong in and of itself | 21 |
| Other objections | 30 |

## VII

The following are some of the more important orders relating to objectors. All the "Confidential Orders" are included.

*"Confidential.*

                        October 10, 117.

*From:* The Adjutant General of the Army.

*To:*      The Commanding Generals of all National Army and National Guard Division Camps.

*Subject:* Conscientious Objectors.

1. The Secretary of War directs that you be instructed to segregate the conscientious objectors in their divisions and to place them under supervision of instructors who shall be specially selected with a view of insuring that these men will be handled with tact

and consideration and that their questions will be answered fully and frankly.

2. With reference to their attitude of objecting to military service these men are not to be treated as violating military laws thereby subjecting themselves to the penalties of the Articles of War, but their attitude in this respect will be quietly ignored and they will be treated with kindly consideration. Attention in this connection is invited to a case where a number of conscientious objectors in one of our divisions, when treated in this manner, renounced their original objections to military service and voluntarily offered to give their best efforts to the service of the United States as soldiers.

3. It is desired that after the procedure above indicated shall have been followed for a sufficient length of time to afford opportunity to judge of the results derived from it, a report of the action taken and the results obtained under these instructions be submitted to the War Department by each division commander. As a result of the consideration of all these reports further instructions will be issued by the Secretary of War as to the policy to be observed in future in the case of conscientious objectors.

4. Under no circumstances are the instructions contained in the foregoing to be given to the newspapers.

(S.) H. G. LEARNARD,
Adjutant General.''

''*Confidential.*                    December 19, 1917.

*From:*  The Adjutant General of the Army.
*To:*    The Commanding Generals of all National Army and National Guard Camps except Camp Grant.
*Subject:*  Conscientious Objectors.

1. The Secretary of War directs that until further instructions on the subject are issued 'personal scruples against war' should be considered as constitut-

ing 'conscientious objectors' and such persons should be treated in the same manner as other 'conscientious objectors' under the instructions contained in confidential letter from this office dated October 10, 1917.

2. Under no circumstances should these instructions be communicated to the newspapers.

(S.) H. G. LEARNARD,
Adjutant General."

"383.2 (Misc. Div.)
March 11, 1918
*From:* The Adjutant General of the Army.
*To:* The Commanding Generals of all National Guard and National Army Divisions.
*Subject:* Conscientious Objectors.

1. You are informed that instructions regarding the segregation of conscientious objectors, contained in confidentia! letters from The Adjutant General of October 10th and December 19th, 1917, should not be construed as requiring the mingling in one group of different classes of conscientious objectors, who, for the good of the service, may better be kept apart.

2. Under no circumstances are the instructions contained in the foregoing to be given to the newspapers.

By order of the Secretary of War:
(S.) H. G. LEARNARD,
Adjutant General."

"June 16, 1918.
*"Confidential.*
*From:* The Adjutant General of the Army.
*To:* All Department and Division Commanders.
*Subject:* Conscientious Objectors—Furloughs.

1. The following confidential instructions, supplemental to instructions from this office, June 1 and June 8, 1918, are furnished for your information and guidance.

2. The Board of Inquiry referred to in paragraph 4, letter of June 1st, is authorized in exceptional cases to recommend furlough for the purpose of engaging in industrial occupations as well as to engage in agricultural work.

3. Such recommendations will be dealt with in the same manner as is provided in orders with respect to agricultural work.

By order of the Secretary of War:

(S.) ROY A. HILL,
Adjutant General.''

"July 30, 1918.

*From:* The Adjutant General of the Army.

*To:* All Department Commanders in the United States; Commanding Generals of all Regular Army, National Army, and National Guard Divisions; Commanding Officers of all Excepted Places; and all Staff Departments.

*Subject:* Conscientious objectors.

1. Letter of instruction, dated June 1, 1918, subject, 'Conscientious objectors; segregation at Fort Leavenworth, Kansas,' is hereby rescinded and the following substituted therefor:

2. By the terms of the Presidential Order of March 20, 1918, men reporting at the training camps under the provisions of the Selective Service Law who profess conscientious scruples against warfare are given an opportunity to select forms of service designated by the President to be noncombatant in character. Commanding officers are instructed to assign to noncombatant service such conscientious objectors as are deemed to be sincere and apply for such service, furnishing such conscientious objectors with a certificate exempting them from combatant service as prescribed in General Orders No. 28, War Department, 1918. Trial by court-martial of those declining to accept such noncombatant service is authorized in the fol-

lowing cases: (a) whose attitude in camp is defiant; (b) whose cases, in the judgment of the camp commander, for any reason, should not await investigation by the board hereinafter referred to; (c) who are active in propaganda.

3. All other men professing conscientious objections, now segregated in posts and camps, i.e., those who, while themselves refusing to obey military instructions on the ground of conscientious scruples, religious or other, have given no other cause of criticism in their conduct, and all who have been or may be tried and acquitted by courts-martial, shall be furloughed as herein directed or transferred to such other stations as may be designated from time to time. Orders for such transfers will be obtained from this office. The commanding officers of all camps or stations will keep these men segregated, but not under arrest, pending further instructions from this office.

4. The same procedure shall be carried out in the cases of men professing similar scruples who may report at posts or camps in the future, when, after due examination by the camp or post commander, such men shall persist in refusing noncombatant service.

5. If there shall be any instances in which the findings of courts-martial at camps or posts in cases involving conscientious objectors shall be disapproved by the Secretary of War, the men concerned shall also be transferred to a segregated detachment of conscientious objectors and examined and reported upon by the Board of Inquiry hereinafter referred to.

6. The Secretary of War has constituted a Board of Inquiry, composed of a representative from the Judge Advocate General's Office (Major Richard C. Stoddard), Chairman, Judge Julian W. Mack, of the Federal Court, and Dean H. F. Stone of the Columbia University Law School. Under no circumstances will conscientious objectors otherwise qualified to perform

military duty be discharged from their responsibilities under the Selective Service Law, but all cases of the character referred to in paragraph two, except those under charges or being tried by court-martial, shall be investigated by this board, who will interrogate personally each individual whose case is so referred to them, and recommend action to be taken. Such men as may be determined by this board to be sincere conscientious objectors as to combatant service, but not as to noncombatant service, shall, on the recommendation of the board, be given an opportunity to select forms of service designated by the President to be noncombatant in character, and such men as may be indicated by this board to be sincere conscientious objectors, both as to combatant and noncombatant service, shall, on the recommendation of the board, be furloughed without pay for agricultural service, upon the voluntary application of the soldier, under the authority contained in the Act of Congress of March 16, 1918, and the provisions of General Orders No. 31, War Department, 1918, provision being made:

(a) That monthly report as to the industry of each person so furloughed shall be received from disinterested sources, and that the furlough may be terminated upon receipt of report that he is not working to the best of his ability; and

(b) That bona fide employment be obtained at the prevailing rate of wages for the class of work in which he engages, in the community in which he is employed.

(c) That no person shall be recommended for such furlough who does not voluntarily agree that he shall receive for his labor an amount no greater than a private's pay, plus an estimated sum for subsistence if such be not provided by the employer, and that any additional amount which may be paid for his services be contributed to the American Red Cross.

7. It is the function of the Board of Inquiry to determine the sincerity of men professing conscientious objections, both as to refusal to perform noncombatant service and also with regard to the performance of combatant service. When the board upon examination believes any man to be insincere in his protestations against the performance of combatant service it will so report to his commanding officer, and such soldier will then be assigned by his commanding officer to any military service and held accountable for its performance.

8. In exceptional cases the board may recommend furlough for service in France in the Friends Reconstruction Unit.

9. Under sub-paragraph (a) General Orders No. 28, work in the reconstruction hospitals of the medical corps is hereby designated as a special class of noncombatant service. It is found that certain men, evidently sincere in their objections to accepting any existing form of noncombatant service, would be willing to accept work in aid of men, who, themselves, are not to be returned to military service. Men assigned to such work should be granted a certificate limiting their service to this particular branch of the medical corps.

10. The attention of all men examined will be especially directed to the opportunities for noncombatant service in the Reclamation Branch of the quartermaster corps, whose activities comprise the laundry service, the salvage service, the clothing renovation service, the shoe repair service, the transportation repair service, and motor truck companies.

11. Any man who is recommended by this board for noncombatant service or furlough, and who refuses to avail himself of the opportunity to be offered to him pursuant to the recommendation, or any man whose furlough shall be terminated as above provided, or for other reasons deemed sufficient by the Secre-

tary of War, shall be required to perform such non-combatant service as may be assigned to him and shall be held strictly accountable under the Articles of War for the proper performance of such service and to strict obedience to all laws governing or applicable to soldiers employed in that status. In the event of disobedience of such laws or failure to perform such service, the offender shall be tried by court-martial, and if found guilty and sentenced to confinement, shall be detained in the disciplinary barracks for the term of his sentence.

12. Pending the final decision in each case as to the disposal of these men, the directions as to their treatment issued from time to time by order of the Secretary of War remain in force. These directions are to be accepted as authoritative interpretations of paragraph three, General Orders No. 28, War Department, 1918, and may be summarized as follows:

(a) As a matter of public health every man in camp, entirely apart from his military status, shall be expected to keep himself and his belongings and surroundings clean, and his body in good condition through appropriate exercise. Men declining to perform military duties shall be expected to prepare their own food.

(b) If, however, any drafted man, upon his arrival at camp either through the presentation of a certificate from his local board, or by written statement addressed by himself to the commanding officer, shall record himself as a conscientious objector, he shall not, against his will, be required to wear a uniform or to bear arms; nor, if, pending the final decision as to his status, he shall decline to perform, under military direction, duties which he states to be contrary to the dictates of his conscience, shall he receive punitive treatment for such conduct. He shall be required to furnish such information and to render such assistance as may be necessary to complete the original entries on all records relating to his induction into the service; but will be informed that such action on his part will not, in any way, prejudice his status as a conscientious objector.

(c) No man who fails to report at camp, in accordance with the instructions of his local board, or who, having reported, fails to make clear upon his arrival his decision to be regarded as a conscientious objector, is entitled to the treatment outlined above.

(d) In the assignment of any soldier to duty, combatant or noncombatant, the War Department recognizes no distinction between service in the United States and service abroad.

13. Regulations for the administration of the furloughs of such men as may be recommended by the board are now being formulated and these soldiers will be removed from the cantonments and stations as promptly as possible.

By order of the Secretary of War:

(Signed) J. B. WILSON,
Adjutant General.''

''October 2, 1918.
*From:* The Adjutant General of the Army.
*To:* All Department and Camp Commanders.
*Subject:* Treatment of Conscientious Objectors.

1. Attention is called to the treatment of men who profess conscientious objections to combatant warfare. The terms of the Selective Service Act indicate that it is the desire of the people of the United States, as expressed in this legislation, to make recognition of the fact that under any draft system men will be called to the colors who profess such objections. The executive order of the President, signed March 20, 1918, sets forth the policy with reference to the administration of the law in this aspect of it. The memorandum of instructions sent out by The Adjutant General on July 30th expresses the desires of the Secretary of

War as to the methods to be pursued in dealing with such men to carry out this policy.

2. There is evidently a wide divergence in the manner in which these men are treated in the different camps and posts. The point at issue is always whether a given man is sincere in his professions. If a man brings evidence from his local board, or from other reputable sources, of his membership in a religious body which is of record as opposed to warfare, or gives evidence of sincerity by his conduct and attitude, it is clearly not the intention, either of the legislation, or of the President's executive order, or the instructions issued by the direction of the Secretary of War that men should be treated, either by officers or enlisted men, pending examination by the Board of Inquiry appointed for the purpose, as if their insincerity and cowardice had already been established. It is not intended or desired that they be pampered or accorded special privileges in any respect not covered by existing instructions; on the other hand, they should not be treated, as in a few cases they have been as men already convicted of cowardice and deceit. It is the experience of the Department that a considerate and tactful attitude toward these men has in many cases resulted in their acceptance, either of noncombatant, or in many cases combatant service, whereas a hectoring and abusive attitude has had an opposite effect.

3. The plans now under way for an enlargement of the Board of Inquiry will make it possible to have these soldiers examined more promptly than has hitherto been the case, and arrangements have also been made for their concentration at points where divisions are not in training.

4. You are directed to notify all concerned.

By order of the Secretary of War:

JOHN S. JOHNSTON,
Adjutant General.''

## VIII

Rule XIV of section 79 of the Selective Service Regulations reads as follows:

"Any registrant who is found by a Local Board to be a member of any well-recognized religious sect or organization organized and existing May 18, 1917, and whose then existing creed or principles forbid its members to participate in war in any form, and whose religious convictions are against war or participation therein in accordance with the creed or principles of said religious organization, shall be furnished by such Local Board with a certificate (Form 1008, sec. 280, p. 225) to that effect and to the further effect that, by the terms of section 4 of the Selective Service Law, he can only be required to serve in a capacity declared by the President to be noncombatant. He shall be classified, however, as is any other registrant; but he shall be designated upon all classifications, forms, records, certificates, and other writings of Local and District Boards in which his name appears by the insertion of a cipher (0) after his name."

Form 1008 reads:
"Local Board for...........
　　　　　　　　　　　　Date.............
This is to certify that.................Order No.
........, Serial No. ......., has been found to be exempt from combatant service and is eligible only to such military service as may be declared noncombatant by the President of the United States.
........................
　　　　　　　　　　Member of Local Board."

The Provost Marshal General reports that 64,693 registrants made claim for noncombatant designation; that 56,830 of such claims were recognized by the Local Boards; that 38,991 of these were classified in Class 1, i. e., as liable for immediate call into service.

The requisitions made by The Adjutant General upon the Provost Marshal General called for delivery by the Local Boards of men qualified "for general military service." Noncombatants, even though in Class 1, obviously did not satisfy such a requisition and hence were never, as such, called to the colors. The few who were found in the Army were either (a) inducted by their Local Boards without regard to the terms of the requisition, or (b) inducted through mistake. It is probably also true that some of these noncombatants later waived their designations and were inducted on the usual call for men qualified for general military service.

The estimate of 3900 (Appendix, I) is believed to be a fair approximation of the total number of accepted and recognized religious and non-religious objectors who actually were in the Army. How many of these were religious-creed objectors holding Form 1008 certificates can not be stated with certainty.

## IX

The Dominion of Canada granted certificates of exemption to 770 objectors. This figure takes no account of the Mennonites and Doukhobors excepted by the Orders in Council. Such men were not required even to register. A certificate from a minister of their church prima facie entitled them to absolute immunity from military service, both combatant and noncombatant. The number of these men was doubtless very large.